To Beth,
for her resilience and good humor
in the face of all of life's
challenges

You can see a lot, just by observing.

Yogi Berra

CHALLENGING THE INCUMBENT

An Underdog's Undertaking

Edward I. Sidlow

Eastern Michigan University

CQ PRESS

A Division of Congressional Quarterly Inc.
Washington, D.C.

CQ Press
1255 22nd Street, N.W., Suite 400
Washington, D.C. 20037

202-729-1900; toll-free, 1-866-4CQ-PRESS (1-866-427-7737)

www.cqpress.com

Printed and bound in the United States of America

07 06 05 04 03   5 4 3 2 1

♾ The paper used in this publication exceeds the requirements of the American National Standard for Information Sciences—Permanence of Paper for Printed Library Materials, ANSI Z39.48-1992.

Cover design: TGD Communications, Alexandria, VA
Composition by Auburn Associates, Inc., Baltimore, MD

Photo credits: *Daily Herald*/Bob Chwedyk, 106; *Daily Herald*/Mark Black, 42; Lance Pressl for Congress, 11, 16, 19, 27, 32, 38, 40, 48, 51, 62, 69, 78, 79, 81, 86, 88, 101, 102, 104, 110–111, 135, 147; Lance Pressl private collection, 20; Scott J. Ferrell, Congressional Quarterly, 21, 44.

Library of Congress Cataloging-in-Publication Data

Sidlow, Edward I.
    Challenging the incumbent : an underdog's undertaking / by Edward I. Sidlow.
      p. cm.
    Includes bibliographical references and index.
    ISBN 1-56802-820-2 (pbk. : alk. paper)
    1. United States. Congress. House—Elections.   2. Elections—Illinois.
3. Illinois—Politics and government—1951–   I. Pressl, Lance   II. Crane, Philip M., 1930- III. Title.
JK1343.I3S53 2004
324.9773'2044—dc21   2003014504

Contents

Illustrations

Preface

I started following Lance Pressl's campaign in the spring of 2000. Lance is a friend and one of my former graduate students, and he had invited me to follow him as he campaigned against Phil Crane, longtime House of Representatives incumbent for suburban Chicago's Eighth Congressional District. The invitation was too good to refuse. Whatever the outcome, it would be valuable material for my legislative politics and elections classes. I also suspected that there might be a good story or two in the experience.

For much of that year, I made the trip from Michigan to Illinois every two or three weeks to connect with the campaign. I also traveled to observe significant events on the Pressl campaign schedule, such as fundraisers and debates. The events reported in the book are based on observation, interviews, and secondary source data. Press accounts of relevant material, as well as nationally archived election data, help to flesh out the story. On the campaign trail, I always carried a microcassette recorder, on which I recorded my own observations and answers to any questions I posed. I conducted lengthy interviews with the candidate and his staff, though, quite frankly, I took my opportunities when and where they were available. To call this a "methodology" is generous, but I am indebted to Richard Fenno, whose work has made it easier to produce this kind of book and have it find an audience in our discipline.

The crux of this story is a long-shot campaign for Congress. Students will read about the benefits that incumbent legislators bring to campaigns, and some of the strategies employed by challengers to overcome those benefits. I hope the highs and lows—the victories and the physical exhaustion and discomfort that characterize these endeavors—are described in a way that resonates with readers. I have tried to humanize the campaign process in recognition of the fact that very real people make extraordinary sacrifices to undertake public service.

The book also provides a glimpse into the campaign industry of consultants, political pros, and intense fund raising that has become such a vital part of twenty-first-century politics. My training as a political scientist helped me place the Pressl campaign in a broader political context and allowed me to highlight behavior patterns common to challengers and incumbents in the circumstances that arise throughout the story. Moreover, the work benefits from, and is informed by, decades of collective scholarship from colleagues around the country. Consequently, the conclusions and generalizations I make are steeped in theoretical and analytical material that is at the heart of our basic understanding of American elections.

I feel it necessary to note that I tried on several occasions to meet with Phil Crane's staff during the time I was researching this project. I did meet Representative Crane at a couple of events and mentioned my work to him. He seemed interested and invited me to call a staff member to set up a meeting, and he indicated that he would be glad to talk politics with me. Unfortunately, my calls were not returned and no appointments were ever made. I regret that, as my insights into the 2000 campaign and election doubtless would have been richer had we been able to visit.

I have incurred many debts while working on this project. The Office of Research and Graduate Studies at Eastern Michigan University provided a grant in support of research. Jessica Heilmann, my Undergraduate Honors Fellow (2000–2001), was a valuable help early on.

Several friends and colleagues provided support and encouragement for which I am also grateful. Ken Janda, my former colleague at Northwestern University, assisted during the project's earliest stages. Captain Michael Jones, a dear friend, read a very early draft of the manuscript and offered valuable encouragement. Monica Eckman read a couple of draft chapters and provided extremely helpful professional advice. I am thankful to each of them. Special thanks are also due to Gerald C. Wright, Indiana University, Eric Heberlig, University of North Carolina at Charlotte, and Jeffrey Gulati, Wellesley College for reviewing the manuscript and providing thoughtful insights and suggestions.

As a young political scientist, I found it somewhat troubling to hear former students say, "I remember your classes because you always told interesting and funny stories." I was, after all, trained to be a university professor, not a storyteller. Over the years, thankfully, I've come to take myself less seriously. If my goal is to teach, and if stories bring material to life for my students, then maybe being applauded for telling stories well is not all that bad. I thank all those students who have listened to my stories.

Obviously, this work could not have been done without the generosity of Lance Pressl. Lance, and his wife, Martha Cotton, tolerated my poking and questioning with charm and good humor. They were always willing to help, and even in the most difficult times, made me feel welcome. Jane Thomas, of the campaign staff, was also very welcoming, generous with her time, and capable of appearing calm during the most chaotic of campaign activities. Simply stated, without these three people, this story could not have been told. I also would like to thank the campaign staff—Brandon, Kim, Pete, and Claude—for their help on my various trips to the district and in follow-up phone interviews.

Brenda Carter, Charisse Kiino, and Elise Frasier, all of CQ Press, have been an absolute pleasure to work with. They quickly grasped what I wanted to do in telling this story and their input greatly improved the book. Elise was particularly helpful and managed to remain remarkably good spirited, while her newborn son, Soren, was thoughtful enough to delay his arrival until after the second draft was completed. Charisse handled my all-too-frequent phone calls at the end of the process with extraordinary patience.

Throughout the writing of this book, my daughter Sarah managed to keep me focused on what's really important. Finally, this book is dedicated to my wife, Beth. She made rough prose smooth, and managed always to be there to help in the midst of juggling professional projects and family responsibilities. Somehow she meets every challenge with a seemingly effortless grace.

E. S.
July 2003
Saline, Michigan

Cast of Characters

in alphabetical order

Martha Cotton   Lance Pressl's wife and primary support person. Busy with her own career, she was still ever present and completely supportive of the campaign.

Phil Crane   Longtime incumbent. Pressl's opposition.

Pete D'Alessandro   Pressl's campaign field director in summer 2000.

Dave Fako   Campaign consultant to the Pressl campaign.

Brandon Hurlbut   First full-time field director for the Pressl campaign.

Jennifer Pohl   Pressl campaign staffer. Joined the campaign in late summer 2000. Hired to do press releases and media relations.

Mike Poleski   Pressl staffer for grassroots organizing. Came to the campaign with D'Alessandro.

Al Pressl   Lance Pressl's father.

Lance Pressl   The challenger. Pressl's story of his campaign against incumbent Phil Crane is the basis of the narrative.

Larry Pressl   Lance Pressl's older brother. Played an important advisory role.

Virginia Pressl   Lance Pressl's mother. Active in the campaign, particularly in securing signatures for nominating petitions.

Molly Ray   Replaced Kim Rogers on finance and fund raising in late summer 2000.

Kim Rogers	Finance director early in Pressl campaign. Brought into the campaign by Hurlbut, with whom she had worked on the Bradley for President campaign.
Jane Thomas	Pressl's campaign manager. With campaign from the beginning.
Claude Walker	Replaced D'Alessandro as field director on the Pressl campaign. Composed the plan followed by the campaign in the final stages of the race.

Campaign Countdown

1999

January Pressl decides to challenge Phil Crane for Illinois's Eighth Congressional District seat.

Fall Pressl and family gather signatures for nominating petitions to place his name on the primary ballot.

October Pressl meets Jane Thomas; she joins campaign as volunteer.

17 November Pressl formally announces candidacy for Congress at Rolling Meadows High School.

7 December First Pressl for Congress fund-raiser.

Jane Thomas officially becomes Pressl's campaign manager.

2000

3 January

15 January Pressl for Congress headquarters opens in Schaumburg, Ill.

Dave Fako, political consultant, hired by Pressl for Congress campaign.

Mid-January

21 March Pressl wins Democratic primary.

Brandon Hurlbut joins campaign staff as field director.

May

Kim Rogers joins campaign as finance director.

June

1 July Palatine Independence Day Parade.

14 July

Pete D'Alessandro replaces Hurlbut.

28 July Mike Poleski joins campaign staff to organize grassroots efforts.

Molly Ray replaces Rogers; Jennifer Pohl joins campaign to handle media relations.

August

4 September Schaumburg Labor Day Parade.

11 September D'Alessandro leaves Pressl campaign.

14 September Claude Walker replaces D'Alessandro.

16 October AARP sponsors Crane-Pressl debate.

20 October

Crane and Pressl meet at League of Women Voters candidate forum.

31 October "Unmasking Phil Crane" press conference.

31 October Pressl radio campaign launched.

7 November Election day.

Prologue
From Political Science to Politics

I HAVE NEVER been able to shake the feeling that, too often, academics take the politics out of political science and in the process remove that which is vital to the discipline. Political science uses scientific and statistical methods to examine a whole range of "living" phenomena that constitute the political and governmental world. For example, political scientists develop simulation models to examine scenarios that might lead to international conflict, or mathematically examine committee preferences of legislators based on such things as region, type of district, length of service, and so on. Others may study whether appointed judges differ in their behavior on the bench from those judges who were elected to their positions. There's a certain sterility that characterizes this kind of work, a sense that the subject is always held at arm's length. It can be interesting at times—and often tells us a lot about political behavior—but it is not necessarily fun.

When I speak about politics, on the other hand, I'm referring to the real world grit that comes with seeking and exercising power. Politics is then both interesting and fun. It conjures up images of stumping for votes, marching in summer parades, and pressing the flesh with voters. It is about sweating and personal sacrifice, about developing a message and style and competing to get that message across. The competition of the political arena can be intoxicating; it was political competition that made politics irresistible for someone like President John F. Kennedy. There's absolutely nothing sterile about politics, about the cold takeout meals in Styrofoam boxes that are eaten by a small group of intimates around a makeshift conference table as campaign strategy is forged. These are the things and images that make politics compelling and real.

This distinction between political science and politics started becoming clear to me in the mid-1970s when I was in graduate school. In fact, I remember quite vividly what inspired this revelation. I was among a group of about fifteen doctoral students who were taking a seminar on legislative politics and behavior with an eminent political scientist. We met weekly, discussed what we had read prior to the session, and considered the variety of questions that were raised by the material or our interpretations of it. It was a spirited group of people in their twenties, who, frankly, probably took themselves too seriously. One week we discussed the concept of representation and at the end of class were told to prepare a three-page paper that defined representation. We were to present our papers at the next class meeting. The assignment allowed us to consider the multifaceted nature of the relationship between an elected official and his or her constituents. I was fairly comfortable with what I had written, having noted how representation amounted to more than a policy agreement between constituent and legislator. I knew that there were important symbolic components to representation, like the fact that the Constitution mandates that citizens be represented in the House on the basis of population, an idea that was reaffirmed by the "one person, one vote" decisions handed down by the U.S. Supreme Court in the early 1960s. I had also noted that certainly part of representational activity in the modern Congress was found in members performing constituent service or bringing projects home to their district.

After some discussion of these issues a fellow student was called on to present his work. He strode to the blackboard with an air of confidence that I could never muster. He then proceeded to cover the entire board with a complex mathematical equation, explaining how each factor in the formula would be operationalized and measured. I was dumbstruck. I found myself thinking, "What the hell is this about?" A long discussion about this "model" of representation ensued. It was scientific, and in my opinion, a great deal removed from reality. I vowed to never allow politics to be left out of my own learning and teaching. This episode clearly drew the distinction between political science and politics for me and helped shape who I am as a teacher. And just when this lesson starts to fade from my mind, the sensation of that afternoon is revisited a couple of times each year when I attend professional meetings in my discipline. There, I always seem to come back to the same question: Why aren't more political scientists doing politics? I recognize the value of good science—and there is a need and place for it in the discipline—but I am also convinced that our teaching and learning can be informed by looking at the political world through the prism of a politician, staffer, or other participant in the game. And in the end, this perspective is what turns students on to politics.

For these reasons, to this day, I am drawn to the work of David Mayhew, Morris Fiorina, and Richard Fenno—three scholars who have made major contributions to our field and who managed to do so while dealing with politics. To be sure, their work is done in a scholarly and systematic way, but it also provides an examination of compelling, important questions about real politicians and how they behave. Some of that behavior is not pretty, but much of it is certainly interesting. Their work, collectively, tells us a great deal about the goals of members of Congress.

Mayhew, for instance, suggests that members of Congress are "single-minded seekers of reelection," whose primary goal is to get themselves reelected.[1] Now, that sounds like politics! Fenno notes that members have three goals: to get reelected, to have influence within their chamber, and to make public policy.[2] It is easy to recognize that the last two goals cannot even begin to be achieved without first getting reelected. First-term members are too busy learning the process to be leading the policy fights and passing significant legislation. First termers actually serve a sort of apprenticeship before becoming productive legislators. Thus, getting reelected is a congressperson's primary goal, but perhaps not as "single-minded" a one as Mayhew suggests. Fiorina takes Fenno's observation a step further, suggesting that members of congress actually work with agencies in the executive branch to deliver programs and services to their constituents, who then reward the legislator for "bringing home the bacon " with reelection.[3] One almost gets the sense that representatives engage in some kind of quiet yet effective unspoken conspiracy to assure their own continued political success.

Of course this is a cynical view of politics, but we live in a cynical age. Many suggest that the reason that congressional incumbents are so difficult to defeat is because they have written themselves so nicely into the game. The perquisites of their office—franking privileges (the ability to send mail to everyone in the district at taxpayer expense); full-time professional staff; access to media; paid travel between Washington, D.C., and their home districts—indeed put incumbents at such an advantaged electoral position that it is nearly impossible to move them out of the chamber. When you add the fact that, by and large, members of the general public have no idea what is going on in Congress, or even who their representative is, and that few constituents bother to vote in congressional elections, the savvy incumbent needs only to win the votes of a small percentage of their total constituency to retain office. If we imagine a turnout of 45 percent in a House election, the incumbent needs to carry only about 23 percent of the vote to continue winning elections! I am not suggesting this is a good thing or a bad thing but simply a plausible explanation of how more than 90 percent of House incumbents manage to get themselves reelected term after term.

And it would be unfair to be critical of representatives for simply wanting to keep their jobs. I do not know too many people who are in a hurry to lose their jobs. Moreover, the job of the legislator is very complex and has a steep learning curve. New members must learn the ropes, so to speak, before they can become effective legislators. Consequently, one can make a very reasoned argument for keeping experienced legislators in office. We also should not underestimate those "goodies" that our veteran members of Congress bring home. Those building projects, road construction and repair programs, water treatment centers, stream bedding projects, and the like all make their home districts better places to live. The projects are also good for local economies. In some respects, then, it might be in our best interest to keep incumbents in office.

The puzzle of whether incumbent reelection success is good or bad is always something that my students find interesting. Although there is no doubt that solid scientific data analysis is critical to gaining a clear sense of the pervasiveness of incumbent success rates, I think this topic resonates for students in part because it brings politics to life. Students initially take the cynical view that all politicians just care about themselves, but when presented with the other realities of the situation they pull back and recognize the conundrum that incumbency success rates present. Though instinctively disturbed by the fact that incumbents seem so unbeatable, students soon come to realize that incumbents bring expertise and potential power in Congress to the electoral situation, and ultimately back to the district. These are traits challengers seldom possess.

Implicitly, the story that is told in this book asks the reader to consider the high success rates of incumbents. Is this fact of American political life desirable? Or not? Is it a case of having to take the bad with the good? Or perhaps, is it just reflective of an electorate that really doesn't care about congressional elections? What kind of work does it take to run against an incumbent? What kind of person would take on such a challenge? Is it worth the personal and financial risks to undertake a challenge that puts a candidate in the position of a long-shot underdog right from the start? Can incumbents ignore their responsibilities and continue to win reelection? Are citizens getting what they deserve if the incumbent does ignore them? After all, citizens certainly seem to ignore Congress. These kinds of questions, it seems to me, offer students a bridge between politics and political science.

An exploration of the business of incumbents and challengers—the real-world grit of politics—is at the heart of this book. The project comes out of an opportunity that one of my former students, Lance Pressl, presented me. He had decided to challenge a longtime House incumbent and invited me along for the ride. That is where this study picks up. I am glad I didn't pass up the chance to step out of the sphere of political science and into the world of politics.

Notes

1. David R. Mayhew, *Congress: The Electoral Connection* (New Haven: Yale University Press, 1974).

2. Richard F. Fenno, *Congressmen in Committees* (Boston: Little, Brown, 1971).

3. Morris P. Fiorina, *Congress: Keystone of the Washington Establishment* (New Haven: Yale University Press, 1977).

The Decision to Run
A Challenger's Bid, an Incumbent's Advantage

ON A BLUSTERY Chicago night in April 1999, the cold rain blowing sideways off Lake Michigan, my wife, Beth, and I stood waiting for a taxicab at the east entrance of the Palmer House Hotel so that we could join two old friends for dinner. We had visited that hotel every April for the past twenty years, and had never waited so long for the bellman to hail a cab. But it was Friday night, the rain was pouring, the wind was howling, and cabs were scarce. There was a cinematic quality to the weather, steam rising from manhole covers in the streets, neon signs reflecting off shiny wet pavement, and the sounds of puddles splashing as cars and buses passed by. In fact, had it been a movie, the director might have picked just such a night to foreshadow the drama in store for us that evening.

Our friends Lance Pressl and his wife, Martha Cotton, lived in Chicago and knew all the trendy restaurants in town. Tonight they had chosen a cute bistro on Clark Street on the near north side for dinner. We arrived at the restaurant an hour late—cold and wet—but we warmed up quickly with a glass of wine and the comfort of reuniting with old friends.

My relationship with Pressl went back nearly fifteen years. I had begun teaching in the political science department at Northwestern University in the fall of 1985, just as Pressl was beginning graduate school there. During that academic year, Pressl was assigned to me as a teaching assistant. Despite our different circumstances, we were fairly close in age and soon discovered that we shared similar interests. Over the course of the year we were, in turn, mentor and student, racquetball partners, friends.

It was not difficult to see that Pressl was different from most graduate students, both in appearance and behavior. He was always impeccably dressed, shirts and trousers were well pressed; he was clean shaven and never had that sleep-deprived, scruffy appearance that seems to be an unwritten prerequisite of most graduate programs. He was also quieter than most graduate students. Graduate students are usually eager to speak up— to let the faculty know how smart they are. Graduate students also tend to be quick to criticize, finding shortcomings in most of what they read, and insinuating that their work will right the wrongs of the research they are examining in their courses. Pressl said rather little, leaving the impression that he knew more than he was saying. When he asked a question, it was likely to be more practical than philosophical, and frankly, he seemed to be floating along in a different orbit than the rest of his classmates. He enjoyed the teaching when he lectured in my class, and interacted well with students; but he knew that he didn't want an academic career. This also differentiated him from the other graduate students who were intent upon landing university faculty positions after graduation. He wanted more action than is typical of a life of teaching and writing, and said on more than one occasion that he would rather do politics than teach it. He seemed always to be figuring, "How can I make things happen?" On more than one occasion I laughingly asserted that I just wanted to be a successful college professor. "But you, Lance Pressl," I would say, "insist upon doing something important."

Indeed, I am a college professor; whether I am successful is for others to judge. This story is about Pressl and the interesting twists and turns of his career. Lance has said that he always found politics interesting and was no doubt bitten by the public service bug before he came to graduate school. Rather than going straight from college to a graduate program, he took a job in June 1979 in the Illinois state government as a budget analyst for the Illinois Bureau of the Budget. This probably explained his unusually professional demeanor as a graduate student and allowed him to make an informed comparison of the world of politics and government on the one hand and academia on the other. He was great at meeting people and thoughtful about keeping up with old contacts. These skills would serve him well as he finished his coursework for his doctorate and began looking for a job.

Indeed, in 1990, after five years of graduate work at Northwestern in political science, he took a position in government affairs with Philip Morris, Inc., as a policy analyst and government affairs specialist. This position put him in regular contact with public officials, and he was stationed in New York, Washington, D.C., and then back in Chicago. But eventually restlessness set in (another of Pressl's characteristics), and he didn't see himself being happy working as a corporate lobbyist or directing a team of other corporate lobbyists, so he left Philip Morris in 1996 to become president of the Chicago Civic Federation, one of the oldest government watchdog groups in the country.

It was no small feat to be hired by that organization. The Civic Federation is a nonprofit, nonpartisan organization that provides research and information to local government while promoting rational tax strategies and efficient government service. The federation also offers potential solutions for improving public expenditures. At the time Lance was hired he was only in his late thirties, and the other candidates being considered were better known and more experienced. While at the federation, Pressl was often mentioned for one or another posts in state or local government. As his network of contacts with the movers and shakers of local politics grew, he became more comfortable with the public role he played as a spokesperson—more good training for a life in politics.

Lance continued to call me regularly, even after I moved to Michigan from Illinois, to seek my advice about the latest career opportunity that had come his way. We had long since moved beyond the mentor-student relationship. During our conversations, he would mention his desire to be closer to the center of action. Although he was involved in government and politics during his time at the Civic Federation, he felt as if he was only on the sidelines of power and influence, and he was itching to be more involved in the game. With each conversation, I felt more and more certain that Pressl would, in fact, "do something important." He was working with a very powerful and impressive crowd—and doing so with relative comfort. To put it bluntly, he seemed to fit in well with the local power elite.

All of this raced through my mind that April night as dinner was ending and Pressl abruptly said, "I have a serious question to ask you both."

"Oh my," I said sarcastically, "he wants to get serious on us."

Lance smiled and continued, "What do you think about my running for Congress?" "Whoa," I said, "this *is* serious." I wanted to blurt out a whole host of questions, including "Are you crazy?" "Which district?" "Is there an open seat?" "Have you been approached by either political party?" "Where will you get the money for a campaign?" "Have you really given this enough thought?" I ordered a cup of coffee instead, and listened to what Lance had to say.

Pressl explained that he and Martha were thinking about moving back to Rolling Meadows, the middle-class northwest Chicago suburb where he had grown up and where his parents still lived. He wanted to challenge Republican representative Phil Crane for his seat in the House of Representatives. Pressl knew it sounded crazy to go after a long-term incumbent—Crane had been in the House since 1969—but he had been looking carefully at the changing demographics of the district. Younger people had been moving into the area, and they were likely to see the world differently than Phil Crane did. Moreover, there was a perception that Crane had been ignoring the district and taking the voters for granted for a long time. Pressl knew it was a long shot, but he thought Crane could be beaten. "We have the opportunity to talk about a new voice for the new millennium," Pressl said. "I can identify with the younger voters, the ones who have moved to the suburbs to raise their families. The median age in the district is thirty-two, and Crane is almost seventy. Crane is also out of touch with the district when it comes to issues." Pressl's typically reserved demeanor was replaced with an air of enthusiasm and passion that I had rarely seen in him before. "Crane doesn't understand the salience of the gun issue to the families who are sending children off to school. He's holding hands with the National Rifle Association, while parents are worried about another Columbine High shooting. Crane doesn't support aid to education; he doesn't support prescription benefits as part of Medicare. He's also out of step on abortion politics."

Pressl went on to note that when Phil Crane was first elected to Congress, folksingers Peter, Paul, and Mary had a radio hit, the AMC Gremlin was a hot new car, and Richard Nixon was in the White House. "Nixon

The challenger, Lance Pressl, with his father, Al Pressl, and wife, Martha Cotton, pictured here on the day Lance formally announced his candidacy at Rolling Meadows High School. Candidates and officeholders need a circle of intimates that they can trust completely. When the Pressl campaign was in its infancy, Lance relied heavily on his family. He was very fortunate to have a supportive wife who was willing to become sole breadwinner while Lance waged his campaign against Phil Crane. Lance's parents, Al and Virginia, offered unyielding support throughout the campaign.

and AMC are both gone," Pressl said matter-of-factly, "and Peter, Paul, and Mary are a nostalgia act. When Crane first went to Congress, I was in junior high school. The world has changed a lot since then. Phil Crane, however, has not changed very much."

My wife and I could tell that Lance was serious—and he could be very convincing. But a gentle reality check was in order. "Lance," I began softly, sounding every bit the professor of political science, "every college student who studies American government knows how difficult it is to defeat an incumbent member of Congress. Incumbent House members who have sought reelection have had an average success rate of 93 percent since World War II, and 98 percent of House incumbents who stood for reelection in 1998 were successful. The benefits of incumbency with respect to name recognition and fund raising alone are enormous. And you're talking about challenging someone who has been in Congress for three decades and is a fixture in this part of the state. Granted, you may think he's a prehistoric fixture, but he is a fixture nonetheless."

"There is one other thing I should mention," Pressl responded. "Representative Crane has a drinking problem. It's widely known in Washington and will likely come out in the campaign. Indeed, among those in the district who are in the know, his problem is a very poorly kept secret. It just seems to me that there is enough here—Crane's views on some key issues, his lack of attention to the district, and his personal behavior—that I think we could beat him." As he spoke, it was clear to me that Lance was already grappling with the issue of Crane's drinking problem and the role it might play in an election. I thought to myself that he was probably wondering about how far he would go in running a negative campaign. Crane's drinking would no doubt come out in any campaign, but the question of how Pressl would handle it was an open one. Perhaps he was already, in a way, in "campaign mode," even as he anticipated running for Congress.

Pressl knew it would be an uphill fight. He was fully aware of all of the difficulties in unseating an incumbent. He knew that fund raising would be a major chore. He even knew that only Republicans had represented that Illinois district since the Civil War. But as my wife sat there in disbelief, wondering to herself how Lance could be thinking about undertaking such a monumental challenge, I told myself that if anyone could pull this off, he could.

The conversation trailed off as we paid the dinner bill and left the restaurant. The rain had let up some, and Lance offered to drive us back to our hotel. In the car we chatted about when we might visit again, and, as always, resolved to get together more often. As my wife and I got out of the car on Monroe Street, Pressl asked one more time, "Do you think I'm really crazy?" My wife and I exchanged glances, and I slowly shook my head. "Maybe not," I said quietly. "Maybe you're not crazy."

On the drive home to Michigan the following day, I thought a lot about a Pressl bid for Congress in the 2000 election. It had been easy for me to report the success rates of House incumbents at dinner the night before; I had just finished discussing Congress in my American government course. Students always seem to become even more cynical about government after they hear how rare it is to defeat a member of Congress who chooses to seek reelection. And when I tell them that the monetary value of a representative's staff and the privilege to use the postal system for free to communicate to constituents in the district amounts to $1.5 million per year, they begin to see why it is so daunting to run against an incumbent. Add to that name recognition and the ability to raise serious money from interest groups, and you've gone a long way toward explaining why so few challengers are successful.[1]

A discussion about the power of incumbency usually produces some student grumbling about system entrenchment and how difficult it is to bring about change. There are always a few in the classroom, however, who shrug their shoulders as if to say, "So what? That's just how it is." So for them I point out that, on occasion, incumbents do lose.

As we continued driving east, away from Chicago, I thought about the incumbents who had lost in recent elections. In 1996, for example, Bob Dornan, who had represented California's Forty-sixth District for eight terms, had been defeated by a Democratic newcomer, Loretta Sanchez. Major changes in the demographic makeup of historically Republican Orange County had contributed to her victory. And if a scandal, such as an alcohol problem, becomes part of the mix, I told myself, the chances of defeating an incumbent increase.[2] The electorate was certainly weary of scandal-ridden politics—and not only because of President Clinton's involvement with a young White House intern, Monica Lewinsky, that had ended in his impeachment in 1998. Six years before that, the public had made it clear that incumbents were not untouchable. In part because they were tired of numerous scandals involving members of Congress, the electorate in 1992 defeated forty-three House members who were running for reelection, as well as five senators. Two years later, thirty-five incumbents—all Democrats—had been ousted. There was also a chance, I thought, that history might, in a fashion, repeat itself. In 1984 Phil Crane's brother Dan, a representative from downstate Danville, Illinois, had lost the seat he had held since 1979 to Terry Bruce, a forty-one-year-old Democrat. In 1983 the House of Representatives had censured Dan Crane for becoming sexually involved with a teenaged congressional page. "Is it possible," I asked myself as we traveled on I-94 through Indiana and into

Michigan, "that Pressl's personal skills, the changing demographics of the Eighth District, and Phil Crane's drinking problem constitute a formula for an upset in November 2000?" I looked over at my wife. She, too, had been deep in thought. And I could tell that she thought Lance was crazy.

Of course, a decision as momentous as whether to run for Congress isn't made during dinner with a couple of old friends. It is, obviously, a decision that cannot be made lightly or in haste. The enterprise is fraught with risk—personal, professional, financial. Most people wouldn't even be intrigued by the idea of running for elective office. Running takes a hard-to-define mix of ambition, desire, ego, and, in most cases, an oddly noble sense of wanting to do good things and help people.

Broadly speaking, candidates for Congress can be put into one of two categories. There are "amateurs," who, by definition, have no political experience, and "pros"—people who have held public office and who very carefully weigh the benefits and drawbacks of launching a run for the House of Representatives or the Senate.[3] Amateurs run for a variety of reasons. Sometimes they are most interested in bringing public attention to a specific issue; winning the election is secondary. Most amateurs, however, have known for a long time that running for office is something they will do at some point in their lives, and they make the decision to run when, for any number of reasons, they determine the time is right.[4] The fact that Pressl was challenging a longtime incumbent no doubt cast the longest shadow over his chances for success against Crane. Indeed, it has been noted that "the vast majority of House challengers barely [manage] to put up a fight against incumbents. They have been characterized as invisible, chronically underfunded, and politically inexperienced."[5]

Pressl was admittedly an amateur. Though successful in his career, he'd had no previous political experience. But at the same time he had always been committed to the idea that at some point he would like to be in elective office. As a student, he was much more taken with the pursuit and exercise of governmental power than with the various models of political behavior that the doctoral curriculum demanded he study. That is to say, he was much more drawn to the practical than the theoretical aspects of politics and political science. His professional career had kept him close to political power. The regular contact with legislators and governors when he was at Philip Morris no doubt kept his interest in electoral politics keen, and that interest would grow further in working for the Chicago Civic Federation on very real issues of public policy. While he did not necessarily see his experience as fitting into some grand strategy that would culminate in a run for Congress, it simply struck him that now was the time to move back home and run. In fact, Pressl would tell you that even as a child he found the notion of elective office "neat." This is probably no great surprise, in that like so many who were born in the 1950s, his earliest political memories were of President John F. Kennedy and the romantic notions of public service that are so much a part of the Kennedy legacy.

Long before our dinner on that April night, Pressl had had several experiences that laid the groundwork for a congressional bid. Perhaps the most relevant occurred in 1974, when Pressl was student council president at Rolling Meadows High School. A young representative came to speak to a student assembly. This was at a time when Democrats and Republicans were every bit as divided on the role of government in solving the nation's problems as they are in the early 2000s. Democrats tended to be more closely aligned with blue-collar workers and unions and favored social legislation to help those in need. Republicans, on the other hand, were supported by big business and stressed self-reliance. In the Republicans' view, government was the problem, not the solution, and conservative Republicans were clamoring for a reduced governmental role. During the assembly, the representative told the students that the free enterprise system was responsible for making all of our lives so good. That system, not the government, was responsible for America's great success. He went on to say that it was the role of government to stay out of the way and let the free enterprise system work. That representative was none other than Phil Crane. Pressl remembers that day with a smile. "Crane also told us that day in May of 1974 that Nixon was not a crook."

Pressl was struck by Crane's visit. He had reason to believe that the free enterprise system was not doing that well by everyone, at least not everyone on his street. The Valentine family next door was having trouble making ends meet. Mr. Smith, who lived across the street from the Pressl house, was unemployed. Lance's father worked two jobs and his mother

25 YEARS AGO, LANCE PRESSL DECIDED WHAT HE WANTED TO DO WHEN HE GREW UP...

U.S. Congressman Phil Crane is welcomed by Student Council President Lance Pressl

1974 Rolling Meadows High School Year Book

BEAT PHIL CRANE!

A shaggy-haired high school student leader, Lance Pressl met a young Republican representative Phil Crane in 1974. This photo appeared in the Rolling Meadows High School Yearbook and was used on an invitation to an early "Pressl for Congress" fund-raiser and was also reprinted in several newspapers. Pressl never forgot his earliest meeting with Crane. Indeed, he spoke of it as planting the seeds that led to his candidacy against Representative Crane more than two decades later.

also worked full time. In the view of Lance Pressl, suburban teenager, the free enterprise system left a lot to be desired. Not surprising, Lance also disagreed with Representative Crane's positive view of President Nixon. In fact, Lance Pressl did not agree with a thing that Crane said to the students at Rolling Meadows High. Shaking hands with the young Republican representative, the shaggy-haired student council president said to himself, "Some day I'd like to run against Phil Crane." The moment was recorded in a photograph on page 22 of *Yearling,* the high school yearbook.

After graduating from high school in 1975, Pressl's interest in politics continued to grow, and he studied political science at Miami University and Northwestern University. With his undergraduate degree in hand, Lance worked for a time as a budget analyst in state government in Springfield, Illinois, before returning to Northwestern University in 1985 to earn his Ph.D. in political science. Then came his work with Philip Morris, where Lance monitored governmental policies related to the various agricultural and corporate concerns of the company. Later, his presidency of the Chicago Civic Federation put Lance in regular contact with state and county officeholders, and he frequently testified at public hearings on tax and fiscal policies.

Certainly, Pressl's interest in things political shaped his early career choices, and when he was at the Civic Federation he considered several possibilities involving greater hands-on political involvement. He was approached about serving on the Illinois Gaming Commission and was asked about running for a seat on the county commission or for the state senate. Most of these inquiries came from people who were plugged into Democratic politics in Chicago or from people with whom he had worked at Philip Morris and the Civic Federation. He was always flattered when approached, but none of these possibilities held any allure. Then, as Lance tells it, he was out jogging on an uncharacteristically mild day in January 1999, and it simply came to him. "Now is the right time to move back home and challenge Phil Crane."

It was much easier, of course, for Lance to say to himself that he was going to challenge Phil Crane in the next congressional election than it was to say it to anyone else. The first person he needed to discuss the idea with was his wife, Martha, and he wasn't at all sure what kind of a reaction he'd get. He was well aware that making a bid for Congress would alter their lifestyle. Challenging Crane would mean leaving their condominium on the near north side of Chicago and moving to suburban Rolling Meadows. Their active involvement in the urban arts community, workouts at their trendy city health club, spur-of-the-moment walks along the lakefront, and dinners at favorite restaurants only a few blocks from home would become a thing of the past. Their professional lives in Chicago would be a long way from the Eighth Congressional District, and a great deal of time would be spent commuting between home and office.

So it was not without trepidation that on that January night in 1999 he broached the topic of running for Congress. During dinner at a favorite Mexican restaurant, Lance asked Martha what she thought of the idea of moving out to Rolling Meadows. Martha responded with a tone of bewilderment in her voice. "Why on earth would we want to do something like that?"

Lance answered, matter-of-factly. "So I can run against Phil Crane."

Martha knew that Lance had political ambitions. He had spoken of his genuine belief in the responsibility of government to help people. She thought he seemed to take the failures of government and politicians personally. He also was troubled by the public cynicism that followed in the wake of Vietnam and Watergate and by the growing mistrust in government that characterized his generation. She knew, too, that he took seriously the call to public service articulated by President Kennedy, his first political hero. She was not surprised, then, that Lance was considering a run for Congress. She had also grown accustomed to making major changes in their lives every few years. In seven years of marriage, Lance had held several different positions with Philip Morris—in three different states—in addition to his current position at the Civic Federation. For her part, Martha also had a varied career history. A master of fine arts from Northwestern University had led to a number of professional acting experiences. Her longtime passion for cooking had resulted in a recently published cookbook. She currently held a senior position with a design research firm. She had an adventurous spirit, and she understood ambition. Martha took a deep breath. "If that's what you want to do, we'll do it."

In a very real sense, this was the beginning of "Pressl for Congress." As Richard Fenno notes in *Home Style*, every member of Congress relies on family or a small, intimate circle of friends for the kind of emotional support that Martha would have to provide if Lance was going to be successful.[6] Martha knew that she must be a full partner in this newest enterprise. Lance would, at some point, have to leave the Civic Federation to devote himself to the campaign full time. She would become the sole breadwinner in addition to playing the role of campaign spouse. Their lives would change dramatically, and Lance knew how lucky he was that she was willing to undertake the challenges that would face them in the year ahead.

The spring months of 1999 were a blur of activity as Pressl took the first preliminary steps toward a candidacy. First, Lance spoke to the people whose opinions he valued and in whom he had complete trust. He started with his older brother, Larry, with whom he was very close. Larry was trained

Martha Cotton, Lance Pressl's wife, holding "Pressl for Congress" campaign paraphernalia. Martha was unwavering in her support of Lance's bid to unseat longtime incumbent representative Phil Crane. As Lance waged his campaign, Martha became accustomed to working two full-time jobs—one in her design research firm and one on the campaign.

in business at Harvard, and now, in his mid-forties, worked in the banking and finance community in Chicago. Lance knew he would be looking to his brother for all kinds of support, emotional as well as professional, if the candidacy were going to happen. Then came conversations with close friends. If his closest confidants told him he was crazy to mount a challenge against Phil Crane, it would be difficult to ignore them and run. In fact, a couple of people did tell him, bluntly, that he was out of his mind. Still, there was enough encouragement (or at least he perceived there to be enough encouragement) for Lance to go forward. Moreover, Lance was also a student of politics who read widely and, probably like most of us, remembered selectively. He knew that incumbents were seldom defeated, but also knew of the rare times the challengers won. No doubt he took heart in comments like those of Mark Andrews, a U.S. senator who lost his bid for reelection in 1980. In talking about his defeat Andrews said, "maybe people just wanted a change." [7] Stories like that and just a little encouragement were enough to move Pressl forward.

Next, casting a wider net, Pressl met with everyone he could think of who might be interested in his campaign or willing to help. He met with people who had run against Crane in previous elections, as well as staffers who had worked on those unsuccessful campaigns. He held meetings in the Eighth Congressional District with local police chiefs, fire chiefs, and

Lance Pressl (right) pictured with his brother Larry (left), nephew Patrick, and mother Virginia. Lance relied heavily on his brother for advice throughout the campaign. Virginia Pressl was a fixture on the campaign trail, attending most of the events that featured her son, the candidate. In the earliest stages of the campaign, it was just Lance, Virginia, and Lance's wife, Martha, gathering signatures for the Pressl nominating petitions. Virginia brought a particular zeal to the task.

members of the school boards. He spoke with political professionals—pollsters, public opinion research experts, and campaign consultants. He met with powerful state officeholders. He sought the blessing of the local Democratic Party organization. He also scheduled meetings with high-profile Democrats in Congress. While he had little in the way of a relationship with members of Congress, his in-laws knew Sen. Edward Kennedy and Rep. Barney Frank of their home state, Massachusetts. This helped in getting appointments with Rep. Patrick Kennedy, D-R.I. (the senator's nephew), who chaired the Democratic Congressional Campaign Committee. That committee, part of the Democratic caucus, helps fund the congressional campaigns of Democratic candidates. He was also able to get a meeting with Rep. Richard Gephardt, D-Mo., the Democratic Party leader in the House. These meetings were preliminary, in part to introduce himself, make sure that the party had not preselected a candidate for the Eighth District in Illinois, and if not, to get the blessing

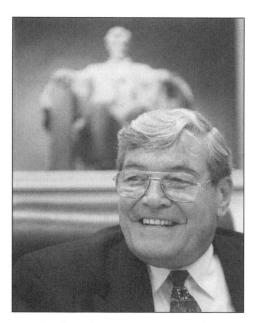

Longtime incumbent representative Phil Crane pictured here in his office in 2000. Crane came to Congress in 1969 as a result of a special election to serve out the unfinished term of another young Illinois Republican, Donald Rumsfeld, who had moved on to serve in the Nixon White House. Crane was consistently reelected throughout the 1970s, 1980s, and 1990s and early in his career would be seen as a leading light among the young conservatives in Washington. Crane also ran for the Republican nomination for president in 1980, fashioning himself as a young alternative to Ronald Reagan.

of the congressional Democratic Party. Lance was graciously treated, encouraged to run, and basically told that if he could show a decent chance of winning, the party would come through with support.

In addition to getting his name out as a potential candidate, there were a number of practical issues that had to be dealt with. Selling the condominium in Chicago and moving to Rolling Meadows was one. Hiring a staff and finding a way to pay them was another. Lance needed someone to run the field operations, someone to serve as finance director, and someone to keep the schedule and manage the office—in space that had to be found and rented.

In the midst of all there was to do, Lance also needed to spend some time alone, reflecting on his views on a variety of public issues and crafting his own political identity. He also had a lot to learn about the Eighth Congressional District and about the issues that were important to the voters. In his most introspective moments, Pressl had to wonder who he was to be running for Congress. Sure, he was an attractive young man in his early forties with a Ph.D. in political science from Northwestern University. His employment record included some interesting positions in state government, the corporate world, and the nonprofit sector. He had grown up in the Eighth District, was a product of the public schools in Rolling Meadows, and his parents still lived in the home where he was raised. He was bright, articulate, and personable. He had the requisite sense of purpose and ambition. He was blessed with a supportive wife and enjoyed the advice of a circle of trusted intimates. But despite the fact that he'd started to drum up other potential supporters, he had never held public office, he was virtually unknown in the whirl of Illinois electoral politics, and he didn't have much money. To put it simply, he had the makings of being yet another young sacrificial lamb to be devoured by Phil Crane, a member of the House of Representatives for over thirty years. This was going to be one heck of a challenge.

Notes

1. Paul S. Herrnson, *Congressional Elections: Campaigning at Home and in Washington,* 3d ed. (Washington, D.C.: CQ Press, 2000), 38–39.

2. As Roger Davidson and Walter Oleszek note, "Nowadays defeating a House incumbent is an uphill struggle, short of a major scandal or misstep." *Congress and Its Members,* 8th ed. (Washington, D.C.: CQ Press, 2002), 61.

3. Ibid.

4. Ibid.

5. Jonathan S. Krasno, *Challengers, Competition, and Reelection: Comparing Senate and House Elections* (New Haven: Yale University Press, 1994), 72.

6. Richard F. Fenno, *Home Style: House Members in Their Districts* (Boston: Little, Brown, 1978), 24.

7. Richard F. Fenno, *When Incumbency Fails: The Senate Career of Mark Andrews* (Washington, D.C.: CQ Press, 1992), 296.

2

The District and the Candidates
The Electoral Context

THE BATTLEGROUND OVER which Phil Crane and Lance Pressl would fight in the 2000 election had changed dramatically during the three decades Crane had served in Congress. The Eighth District had been redrawn three times and expanded to the west and north.

The district had also grown tremendously in population over those thirty years. Indeed, it was one of the fastest-growing districts in the Midwest. When Phil Crane came to Congress in the late 1960s, he represented the solidly Republican Thirteenth Congressional District. There were moderate Republicans in the north shore suburbs of Evanston, Wilmette, Kenilworth, and Winnetka and a substantial Jewish population in Glencoe, and these groups were less receptive to Crane's militant conservatism. The district also contained the suburb of Skokie, which had a large Jewish population, including an active group of Holocaust survivors, and Democratic candidates tended to run very well in that area. Had some of the wealthier Republican areas been districted out of the Thirteenth District and the overwhelmingly Democratic town of Skokie remained in Crane's district, he would have likely found himself facing a serious challenge from a liberal Democrat for the seat in the 1970s. But this did not happen. Fortunately for Crane, the 1972 redistricting removed the more moderate north shore communities from his district, and Chicago's powerful Democratic mayor Richard J. Daley bargained to have Skokie attached to a district that included the northern edge of Chicago and ensured holding onto a Democratic seat.

In the 1970s, and because of further redistricting in the 1980s, all of the less solidly Republican areas were excised from Crane's district, which was

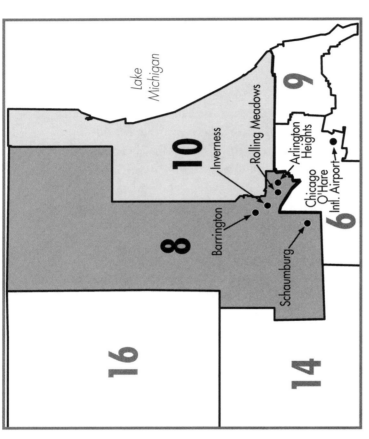

The Eighth Congressional District in Illinois, 2000. The district runs from the northwest Chicago suburbs, near Chicago O'Hare International Airport, all the way north to the Wisconsin border. The district's population has come to include a growing Latino community in the more woodsy lake towns in the north. Schaumburg, one of the larger suburbs, is home to the Woodfield Mall, prototype of the large two-story indoor shopping centers that dot the suburban landscape nationally. Whereas Schaumburg has all of the congestion of a suburban shopping destination, Barrington and Inverness are among the wealthier suburban Chicago towns. The lake towns in the northern part of the district are a popular summer recreation area.

now renumbered the twelfth. This district was transformed into something that more closely resembled the Chicago of the great midwestern plains than that of the ethnic city with big shoulders. That is, it was an area populated by hardworking, churchgoing Midwestern businesspeople, farmers, and their families, rather than the storied streets of Al Capone and the urban life so often associated with Chicago. The twelfth was the district of the famed Paul Harvey radio news, the popular homespun, conservative radio voice that would later become even better known with his "The Rest of the Story" radio feature. It was also the kind of place where one would find the Sears catalog on living room coffee tables. It was an optimistic, conservative area that was well personified by its representative, Phil Crane. This kind of Chicago of the plains extended its orbit downstate, where Ronald Reagan grew up, and provided the foundation for Reagan's characteristic, anything-is-possible optimism. In fact, Reagan carried nearly 80 percent of the vote for president in this district in 1980 and 1984, and Crane was routinely reelected by similar margins.

Further redistricting moved Representative Crane into what was the Eighth District in the 1990s. The eighth was still quite Republican, and certainly conservative. In this district George Bush beat Bill Clinton 47–31 percent in 1992, with Ross Perot garnering an impressive 22 percent as an independent candidate. In 1996 Bob Dole beat Bill Clinton 49–41 percent there, with Perot winning 9 percent.

By 2000 the district had changed quite dramatically from the Thirteenth District that originally sent Phil Crane to Congress. The district had gained nearly 10 percent minority population, a population that traditionally votes in favor of Democratic candidates. Moreover, the percentage of voters willing to support an independent candidate in 1992 and 1996 was also heartening to Democrats, because it showed that voters in the district could be moved out of the Republican camp if they had an attractive alternative. Indeed, both of these factors played into Pressl's decision to challenge the most senior Republican in the House of Representatives in 2000.

In fact, the Eighth District of 2000 gave Democrats several things to be hopeful about. There was a larger population of young families who had left the city for the good school systems and safe neighborhoods of the suburbs. These voters were likely to favor more gun control and aid to disadvantaged citizens than were older residents of the district. Moreover, the tremendous growth in the district brought in more renters and hourly workers who would also be more likely to support a Democratic candidate—particularly one who would eagerly speak to the needs for affordable housing and health care. The largest city in the district, Schaumburg, is home to one of the first mega-shopping malls, a prototype for the many two-story indoor shopping centers that dot the suburbs nationwide. It is the kind of center that would attract sophisticated shoppers, those who might find the politics of Phil Crane a bit dated.

Crane though, had also benefited from some changes in the district. The Eighth District is home to several large corporations, including Motorola, Sears, and Zurich American Life Insurance. The expansion of business and technology into these Northwest Chicago suburbs brought well-educated and upper-middle-class professionals to the area. The conservative views of these new residents blended almost seamlessly into the Republican voting patterns that had sent Crane to Congress for so many years. Always a friend to business and management, Crane could count on support from that group of constituents. Additionally, the towns of Streamwood, Arlington Heights, and Palatine retained their largely Republican flavor and could be counted on to continue supporting Phil Crane.

Suburban sprawl brought commercial opportunities—and a number of challenges. Strip malls, restaurants, automobile dealerships, hotels, and movie theaters sprang up to meet the needs of the community and created jobs. But rapid growth put a burden on roads and infrastructure and brought a host of environmental problems. Congestion was a growing concern of the residents of most of the district, and a major problem for the residents of Lake County in the northern part of the district, which had been primarily rural only a short time ago. Young families who had moved from the city to the suburbs to raise their children on what they had hoped would remain quiet, tree-lined streets, were finding that much of the district was changing from an idyllic *Leave It to Beaver* environment to a faster-paced world. Two working parents, an SUV in the driveway, and furniture from the new, enormous Ikea store typified another

The modest Rolling Meadows home where Virginia and Al Pressl raised their sons, Larry and Lance. Al and Virginia still live in this house, pictured here in late summer 2000 with windows plastered with "Pressl for Congress" signs and yard signs posted in the front lawn. The yard signs would become the subject of a Chicago Tribune *article near election day.*

major new component of the younger, more heterogeneous constituency that Phil Crane now represented.

Lance Pressl saw himself as the person who could best represent the residents of this rapidly changing district. He had grown up in the small bedroom community of Rolling Meadows, where his parents still lived in their small, 1950s ranch house. Lance and his older brother, Larry, had gone to public school. Lance was a star player on the Rolling Meadows High School football team and president of the student council. Lance hoped that these experiences, along with the career choices he'd made since his graduation from Northwestern University, would add up to a resume that would seem familiar to the upwardly mobile professionals who were moving to the suburbs.

As a political scientist, Pressl knew that political party affiliation among younger voters was much more fluid than the long-held Republican Party identification of those voters who initially put Phil Crane in office in 1969. He also knew that the younger parents in the district, given the times in which they were raised, were likely to be less conservative than Crane on a number of social issues. As a fiscal moderate and a social liberal, Lance thought his candidacy was one that these new families in the Eighth District could identify with. Phil Crane, on the other hand, could be painted as woefully out of touch. Moreover, it was reasonable to assume that growth in the minority communities in the district would bode well for a Democratic candidate.

Nevertheless, Phil Crane, the Republican, was the incumbent. He had been sent to Congress as a result of a special election in 1969, filling the seat vacated by Donald Rumsfeld, who had accepted a position in the Nixon administration. Crane was easily reelected to the House of Representatives in 1970. Seen as a rising star among conservative Republicans, his name was often mentioned along with those of other young conservatives such as Rumsfeld, Jack Kemp, and Robert Michel as part of the future of the right wing of the Republican Party. Indeed, Rumsfeld, Kemp, and Michel moved quickly to assume positions of political leadership.

Rumsfeld's illustrious postcongressional career included stints as director of the Office of Economic Opportunity and assistant to President Nixon (1969–1970), counselor to the president (1971–1972), U.S. ambassador to NATO (1973–1974), White House chief of staff under Gerald Ford (1975–1976), and secretary of defense under President Ford (1975–1977) and President George W. Bush (2001–). After leaving the House of Representatives, Jack Kemp served in the cabinet of the first President Bush as secretary of housing and urban development. He was also on the ticket as Bob Dole's vice presidential running mate in 1996. Robert Michel, a member of Congress from Illinois, had a long career in the House as an influential member of the Republican caucus and served for many years as the Republican Party leader in the House of Representatives. Crane's career path, however, was different.

Crane was born in 1930 and raised on the south side of Chicago. He was the second of five children, and his father, Dr. George Crane, was the author of a nationally syndicated newspaper column entitled, "The Worry Clinic." Dr. Crane also had a radio program that aired on Chicago's powerful WGN radio, on which he gave medical advice and served as "a pillar of conservative thought." [1] His brother Dan grew up to win a congressional seat from downstate Illinois, and another brother almost won a seat in Congress from Indiana. Clearly, Crane came from a successful, high-visibility family.

After earning an undergraduate degree in 1952 at Hillsdale College in Michigan, Crane started graduate school at the University of Michigan. His study was interrupted by two years of military service in the U.S. Army from 1954 to 1956. Upon discharge from the service, Crane attended Indiana University, where he earned an M.A. (1961) and Ph.D. in history (1963). Crane and his wife, Arlene, were married in 1959 on Valentine's Day and would go on to have eight children. He was a history professor at Bradley University in Peoria, Illinois, from 1963 until 1967 and served as the director of schools at Westminster Academy in Northbrook, Illinois. He also published his first of three books, *The Democrats' Dilemma,* in 1964. It spoke to the liberal orthodoxy that Crane believed had taken over the Democratic Party. In large part, the book linked that liberalism to socialist elements that he suggested were present in American labor.[2] During this period, Representative Crane worked for the Republican Party as a public relations expert for the Goldwater for President campaign, and from 1964 to 1968 he was an adviser to Richard Nixon, who would run successfully for president in November 1968. It was after Nixon's successful bid for the presidency that Crane became active in electoral politics. Early in his congressional career Crane was characterized as a "conservative intellectual . . . an increasingly common feature of American political life." [3] It is probably instructive to note that this was at the same time that Henry Kissinger, a Harvard professor of political science, enjoyed considerable influence in the Nixon administration and William Buckley was gaining notoriety as a conservative thinker with his work at the *National Review.* This tradition is carried forward today by George Will at ABC News and *Newsweek* and William Kristol, editor of the *Weekly Standard.* In the mid-1980s the *Almanac of American Politics* referred to Crane as "handsome, congenial, loyal to his beliefs but full of good-hearted camaraderie." [4] This suggests that Crane was certainly likable and enjoyed positive relationships with his colleagues but that he was also perceived as somewhat rigid in his conservative views.

Crane came to Congress in 1969 supporting the war in Vietnam and opposing abortion rights. He was in favor of reducing the size of government in Washington, D.C., and reducing the activity of the federal government in state and local affairs. The primary role of the federal government, Crane believed, should be in national defense and foreign policy. He was also a firm believer in the free enterprise system. A loyal Republican, Crane stood with Richard Nixon to the bitter end of the Watergate scandal in 1974.

After being reelected to the House in 1972, 1974, 1976, and 1978, Phil Crane began a quest for the 1980 Republican Party presidential nomination. Spending considerable time over the course of a year in New Hampshire during the winter of 1979 until the primary in February 1980, it appeared to many observers that Crane saw himself as a young alternative to Ronald Reagan, who Crane thought was too old to run successfully for the presidency.

Though Crane and his supporters believed that his conservative record would be appealing to Republicans, the "Crane for President" movement never really caught on in New Hampshire. Ronald Reagan won that very important primary with 49.8 percent of the vote. George Bush, Howard Baker, and John Anderson all finished ahead of Crane, who garnered only 1.8 percent of the votes in New Hampshire. Many people have suggested that after his failed bid for the presidency in 1980, Crane's demeanor changed, and he never regained his vitality. Although he won every subsequent election to the House of Representatives and was a loyal partisan, he never held any real leadership positions.

There was a possibility, however, that should he be reelected in 2000, Phil Crane might finally wield some influence in the House. If the Republicans retained control of the chamber, which appeared likely, Crane would be next in line to chair the powerful Ways and Means Committee. This influential and desirable committee considers legislation having to do with taxes, trade, Medicare, and Social Security and has long been considered a base of considerable legislative power in the House of Representatives.

The current chair was stepping down. As the next most senior member of the Republican Party on the committee, Crane was the logical choice to become chair. But Rep. Bill Thomas, a Republican on the committee from California, had made it known in the spring of 2000 that he might challenge Crane for the chairmanship. And, of course, Crane was facing a challenge for his seat in the House from a young Democratic candidate, Lance Pressl.

Crane and Pressl differed in many ways. Crane was a political veteran who would soon be seventy years old. Pressl was a forty-two-year-old political novice. Crane's father had been a physician and the host of a popular conservative radio program in Chicago. Pressl had grown up in a middle-class family with two working parents. Crane's family had been active in Republican Party politics. Pressl's parents were traditional Chicago Democrats, though neither was politically active. Although Virginia Pressl, Lance's mother, remembered handing out campaign literature and buttons for Adlai Stevenson during his presidential campaigns in the 1950s and working enthusiastically for the election of President Kennedy in 1960, Mr. and Mrs. Pressl usually limited their political activities to voting. They did, however, pass on a strong sense of the importance of government and civic affairs to their two sons.

The two candidates also differed significantly on most of the major issues of the day. Pressl, for example, favored campaign finance reform, Crane did not. Crane was in favor of privatizing Social Security, Pressl was not. Pressl thought that prescription drug benefits for senior citizens should be incorporated into Medicare, Crane did not. Crane was against abortion rights, Pressl was for them. Crane was opposed to a patient's bill of rights, Pressl supported one. Pressl was in favor of stronger gun control measures, Crane was satisfied with current gun laws. Crane favored corporate tax cuts, Pressl did not. Pressl was concerned about environmental protection and favored increasing the minimum wage, Crane typically supported positions sympathetic to business and industry. Crane's legislative interests focused on foreign trade policy, while Pressl's legislative agenda highlighted early childhood development programs and health care for seniors. The different views Crane and Pressl held meant that the voters of the Eighth District would have a clear choice in November, and Lance pointed that out at every opportunity during the campaign.

Ironically, one issue that was uppermost in the minds of the district's residents was something neither candidate could address—traffic congestion in the booming growth areas where Cook and Lake Counties meet in the district. "All politics truly are local," Lance would muse after being questioned about his plans for improving the flow of traffic in that area. Beyond helping with project funding, traffic congestion is something that

Rep. Phil Crane addressing an outdoor event in Rolling Meadows in the summer of 2000. Lance's home town was one of the suburban communities where he hoped the themes of his campaign would be well received.

members of Congress, Republican or Democrat, veteran or newcomer, can do very little about since these issues are typically controlled by state and local political bodies.

Throughout Crane's years in Congress, he enjoyed strong support from insurance companies, the pharmaceutical industry, medical professionals, hospitals and nursing homes, the securities and investment industry, the banking community, and groups such as the Chamber of

Commerce, local real estate boards, and the Automobile Dealers Association. Other sectors of the business community routinely contributed money to his campaigns, as did the National Rifle Association, groups associated with the Christian Coalition, and those connected to the anti-abortion movement.

As the campaign unfolded, much of Pressl's support came from groups that typically oppose conservatives like Phil Crane. All of the major labor unions in the Chicago metropolitan area endorsed Lance. The AFL-CIO; Illinois Federation of Teachers; United Automobile Workers; American Federation of State, County, and Municipal Employees; International Brotherhood of Electrical Workers; Sheet Metal Workers; and Northeastern Illinois District Council of Carpenters all sent statements of support to his campaign. In addition, issue groups such as the Illinois chapter of the National Organization for Women, Voters for Choice, Sarah Brady Handgun Control Group, Planned Parenthood, and Citizen Action Council all lent public support to Pressl's effort to unseat Crane. Of course, Lance would have loved visible support from the Democratic Congressional Campaign Committee, but he knew that he would have to prove his electability first.

During the campaign Crane and Pressl supporters would emphasize not only the different positions their candidates were taking on the issues, but also the images the candidates presented to the voters. Crane's experience and seniority were critical to many of his constituents. "I will be at my polling place bright and early on Election Day to cast my vote for Congressman Phil Crane," wrote a resident of the Eighth District from Barrington. "After thirty years of standing up for the citizens of Illinois in Washington, he is poised to become the next chairman of the House Ways and Means Committee. Illinois will be in a great position after this election. We will be sending an Illinois dynamic duo to Congress—Speaker of the House Denny Hastert and Chairman Crane of Ways and Means. They will be real-life congressional super heroes standing up for the people of Illinois." [5]

Pressl supporters touted their candidate's youth and enthusiasm. "You have to see it to believe it! Lance Pressl, Democratic candidate running for the Eighth District seat is literally doing just that," wrote a voter from

Schaumburg. "At every local parade Lance and his volunteers have participated in this summer (Bartlett, Island Lake, Lindenhurst, Gurnee, Hoffman Estates, Rolling Meadows, Grayslake, etc.), viewers found him literally running from the beginning to the end of each parade. To watch him is amazing. He runs from side to side of the parade route doing his best to greet everyone at the parade. That's the kind of representative the people in the Eighth District need: a young, energetic doer, thinker, communicator, people-oriented representative, who will work hard for his constituents. The Eighth District deserves a candidate like Pressl. Come November, I know who I'm voting for. How about you?" [6]

All of this would come later, of course. Right now, Pressl had to get started.

Notes

1. Michael Barone and Grant Ujifusa, *The Almanac of American Politics 1986* (Washington, D.C.: National Journal Inc., 1986), 419.

2. Phillip M. Crane, *The Democrats' Dilemma* (Chicago: Henry Regnery Company, 1964).

3. Michael Barone, *The Almanac of American Politics 1972* (Boston: Gambit Publishers, 1972), 216.

4. Barone and Ujifusa, *The Almanac,* 419.

5. N. E. H., "Crane Is Next in Line," Letter to the Editor, *Daily Herald,* October 12, 2000.

6. E. N., "Energetic Candidate," Letter to the Editor, *Daily Herald,* September 7, 2000.

The Early Days
Building Support

STARTING A POLITICAL campaign is akin to starting a new job. It's difficult to know exactly what you should be doing or how you should be doing it. For Lance Pressl, the early days of the campaign were filled with uncertainty. He was well aware of the enormity of facing off against a thirty-year congressional incumbent, and he couldn't begin to imagine the emotional ups and downs that would mark his foray into electoral politics.

Having made the decision to run in the spring of 1999, Pressl had about one year to pull together a campaign organization and strategy before the primary election. On March 21, 2000, Lance would compete in a primary election against any other potential Democratic candidates who wanted to run against Phil Crane for the Eighth Congressional District seat. After the primary there would be about seven months to campaign before it would all be over—win or lose. On November 7, 2000, the race for the presidency, contests for one-third of the Senate seats, representation in all 435 House districts, and a host of state and local elections would all be decided.

Through the spring and summer months of 1999, Lance began to lay the groundwork for the upcoming primary campaign as he continued to serve as president of the Chicago Civic Federation. He met with local party officials in the Eighth District to indicate his intention to seek the party's nomination as its congressional candidate. Although the district had no strong Democratic Party organization, Lance thought it was important to pay homage, and he was careful not to alienate anyone who might be willing to help him as the campaign got under way. In particular, he paid attention to Democratic Committee member Victory McNamara, an elected party official for the Eighth District, and to the Wheeling Township commissioner, Patrick Botterman. Given the strength of the Republican Party in the area, these two local politicians were among the most powerful, visible, and successful Democrats in the district, and Pressl felt he had to "pass muster" with these folks to proceed.

These new contacts helped Lance familiarize himself with the local party. But he also had some long-term informal contacts he could draw upon. Indeed, he had managed to keep in contact with the district, and the people in it, throughout his adult life, and he had done so in a variety of ways. When he was in graduate school at Northwestern and later while working in Chicago, he had taught American government courses at Harper Community College, which operates a large campus in the district. He also stayed in touch with friends from high school, and they would keep him up to date on news of mutual acquaintances and noteworthy events in the area. Finally, while at the Civic Federation, Lance broadened the federation's activities to include the suburbs. In particular, he worked with suburban communities on property tax issues and strategies for getting more money into schools. His work with the federation in that regard—though not undertaken with any future political candidacy in mind—not only familiarized him with the issues facing suburban communities but also kept him in contact with people in the Eighth District.

Nevertheless, Pressl was pretty much on his own as he formulated his plans to enter the congressional race. As Paul Herrnson has pointed out, the United States has witnessed "the development of a candidate-centered congressional election system. In the United States, candidates, not parties, are the locus of most campaign activity." [1] Given the lack of Democratic Party organization in the Eighth District, Pressl's was truly a candidate-centered enterprise.

Unlike other democracies, where political parties recruit and select candidates for the national legislature, in the United States congressional candidates are largely self-selected. Of course the party might provide financial support, organizational help, and campaign workers, but this is typically reserved for open-seat elections that the party believes it has a chance to win. An open-seat election has no incumbent running, and this certainly was not the case in the Eighth District. If Pressl could generate enough support and convince the Democratic Party that he had a chance to beat Phil Crane, then the party might join the fight with funds and other assistance. Until that happened, he was on his own. During the summer months, Pressl took whatever time he could to study the issues, familiarize himself with Crane's record, and speak with friends, professional contacts, and potential supporters to alert them to his upcoming bid to unseat the long-term incumbent. Because he still had a full-time commitment to the Civic Federation, however, the hours that he could devote to the campaign were limited.

As fall approached it became time for Pressl to gather signatures for the nominating papers that would be filed with the board of elections. The rules governing primary elections are typically made by state party organizations. In most states, the parties' congressional candidates are selected in primary elections, but there is no fixed number of signatures required across the districts to place a candidate's name on the ballot. The number of signatures that were necessary to place a candidate's name on the primary election ballot for the 2000 congressional primary in the Eighth District of Illinois was 475.

Getting the signatures was a family endeavor. Lance walked door-to-door, sometimes alone, sometimes with a volunteer, asking residents to sign his nominating petition so that he could challenge Phil Crane for Congress. Lance's wife, Martha, and his mother, Virginia, also worked to gather signatures. Virginia brought particular zeal to the task. One of her most successful tactics was deployed in supermarket parking lots. She would quickly move to help people load their groceries into the trunks of their cars. As the customer was busy thanking her, Mrs. Pressl asked if he or she was a registered voter in the Eighth Congressional District. If the answer was "yes," Virginia produced a nominating petition and informed the customer that her son, who was running for Congress, needed to gather signatures to have his name placed on the primary ballot. The method was virtually foolproof.

While Virginia's tactics caused Lance some consternation, he was more concerned about the disqualification of signatures. He had heard stories about strong campaign organizations challenging signatures on

Lance Pressl with his mother, Virginia, and father, Al, leading the Pressl contingent at a Memorial Day rally. Al and all Rolling Meadows veterans were honored with medallions at the ceremony. The Pressl team participated in as many rallies and parades as possible, and always with a group of enthusiastic volunteers. Lance always found the parades energizing (though tiring) and typically enjoyed a warm reception from the crowd.

nominating petitions for a variety of picayune reasons. Signatures might be challenged, for example, because a voter abbreviated certain parts of his or her legal address, as in "R.M." for Rolling Meadows, or "Pal." for Palatine. He had also heard of signatures being challenged because they didn't match exactly the signature on an old voter registration card.

In the wake of the 2000 presidential election it is ironic to think about this small congressional campaign operation worrying about signature challenges in October of 1999. Of course, Pressl had no way of knowing that ballot formats, hanging chads, and charges of disenfranchisement in the state of Florida would be the stuff of such dispute that the country would not know who the next president was going to be for more than a month after election day. However, as Lance put it, "we were very green and flying by the seat of our pants. We weren't really sure about anything that we were doing." In the end, to be safe the Pressl team gathered nearly 2,300 signatures, almost five times the number needed for a spot on the primary ballot. And, as it happened, Lance ran unopposed in the March 21, 2000, primary.

It was in the autumn before the primary election that Pressl met a person who would come to play a central role in his campaign. Jane Thomas, a recently retired college professor, was fairly active in local politics. Her interest in politics—though not her political leanings—probably had something to do with her father. In the Connecticut town in which she was raised, Jane's father had been president of the local chapter of the Italian American Republican Club when Jane was twelve. Many years later Jane volunteered for the Democratic Party when the national nominating convention was held in Chicago in the summer of 1996. She also volunteered on the campaign of a Democratic candidate who ran from a state senate district that covered much of the same territory as the Eighth Congressional District. Though her candidate lost, Jane learned a great deal about the people and places in that area. Although Jane did not have many political contacts, she could marshal an army of dedicated volunteers from the community college where she had worked for so many years. Her friends were like-minded social liberals who would gladly (and later did) turn out to work on defeating Phil Crane.

A longtime resident of the Eighth District, Jane had voted against Phil Crane at every opportunity and disagreed strongly with virtually every issue position he held. Lance met Jane at a political caucus of the Women's Leadership Council that was hosting a forum attended by several political candidates. The purpose of the caucus was to give advice about how to run a political campaign. When Jane learned that Lance was challenging Phil Crane, she was ready to sign up. Not long after that initial meeting the two of them decided over lunch to work together.

When Jane Thomas signed on to the Pressl campaign, she was a sixty-three-year-old woman whose youthful appearance gave no hint of her age. She brought to the enterprise what she characterized as a "we're gonna do it" attitude, which was in keeping with Lance's view. Jane describes herself as "one of those kind of people who operates under the credo that if you believe strongly that something will happen, then it will;

Jane Thomas, the tireless campaign manager, with her grandchildren, all decked out in their "Pressl for Congress" garb. There was a family feel about the Pressl campaign, as staff members and volunteers often brought their children and grandchildren to parades and rallies. This was part of the Pressl strategy to stress youth and vitality in the campaign.

provided that you work your ass off to make it happen." She knew that they were working against long odds, but she expected to win in November. A specialist in early childhood development, she started the preschool at a community college located in the Eighth District and eventually joined the college faculty. Over the years her professional responsibilities and activities had given her opportunities to advocate for children's issues with politicians and officeholders, and she became comfortable interacting in the political arena. In the months ahead Jane's professional training would serve Lance well. She provided access to community practitioners who were knowledgeable about and interested in children and family issues. In addition, her expertise regarding issues relating to children helped inform Lance's own views on policies involving child care and education. These were the kinds of kitchen table issues that Lance expected to strike a chord with the young families who had moved into the district. Issues like these—ones that hit close to home and affected daily life in the district—were what Lance viewed as his political bread and butter.

With Jane signed on as a volunteer, the Pressl campaign now consisted of Lance, Jane, Martha, and Virginia. Jane worked from home developing databases of potential supporters, contributors, and volunteers. She also began contacting various organizations such as local chapters of the Jaycees, Kiwanis, Lions Club, and similar groups to see if they would be willing to have Lance speak at their meetings. Additionally, she contacted school board members, police chiefs, fire chiefs, and any other local officials that she could to set up meetings for Lance. During the fall, the campaign "organization" also made plans to formally announce Lance's candidacy sometime in mid-November.

Pressl wanted the formal announcement of his candidacy to take place at his alma mater, Rolling Meadows High School. The school principal, however, was not eager to give the impression that the school was endorsing a particular political candidate. Even though Lance was a 1975 graduate of Rolling Meadows High and would soon receive an Outstanding Alumni Award, the principal was reluctant to grant permission for the announcement until a member of the school board called to persuade him that there might be educational merit in having a congressional candidate visit the high school and meet with students. At the last minute the principal acquiesced. Good thing—because the Pressl campaign did not have a backup plan.

Before the announcement, which was Jane's first big event since joining the team, Lance and Martha enlisted the services of a graphic artist and friend, Jodi Forlizzi, to produce some campaign literature and a logo, buttons, and a banner proclaiming "Pressl for Congress." (Jodi generously donated her time and expertise.) Martha thought the banner should hang behind Lance in the auditorium when he announced his candidacy for Congress. The drama teacher thought otherwise. "No banner," he insisted.

"The banner should be pinned to the stage curtain behind the podium when Lance makes his announcement," Martha countered. For reasons not entirely clear to Martha (though she suspected the drama teacher didn't want pinholes put in the new stage curtain), the drama teacher

Lance Pressl announcing his candidacy for the congressional seat representing the Eighth District in Illinois. Lance made the announcement at his alma mater, Rolling Meadows High School. He would receive an Outstanding Alumni Award later in the year. The "Pressl for Congress" banner hanging behind the candidate represents a victory for Lance's wife, Martha, in the rough and tumble world of campaign politics.

held firm to his stance. But Martha can also be persistent, and in the end the candidate's wife won the battle of the banner. A small victory perhaps, but a victory nonetheless.

Lance had no idea if there would be any press coverage of his announcement, or what the students' reaction would be. But on November 17, standing in front of a banner that bore his name, Lance Pressl made it official: he was running for Congress. Lance spoke for about ten minutes, hitting on key social issues and noting where he differed with Phil Crane. He also visited several classes, chatted with students about his time at Rolling Meadows High, and answered questions about why he wanted to run for Congress. Members of the debate team grilled him, wanting "yes or no" answers to some very complex questions. They also took Pressl to task for having worked for Philip Morris. Lance was prepared for the

Philip Morris question, responding that he had not accepted campaign contributions from his former employer and that he's always been troubled by several of the issues surrounding tobacco and its use. However, he also spoke to the diversity of Philip Morris, Inc., and pointed out that 90 percent of the homes in America had Philip Morris products in them, including all of the Kraft macaroni and cheese that small children loved. He told them that Philip Morris was not only Kraft foods, but Post cereal, Toblerone chocolate, and Tang drink mix as well. Lance also spoke to the commitment to philanthropic giving that characterized the Philip Morris companies and the significant amount of money that they gave to the arts and hundreds of charities. Finally, Lance told the students that he could not have thought about running for office without the lessons in practical politics that he learned while working at "P.M.," Inc. Lance admired the high school debaters who let him have it. He remembered meeting Phil Crane at Rolling Meadows High School and thought about how much he would have relished the opportunity to challenge Crane as the students were challenging him on this day.

As it happened, the press coverage of Pressl's announcement was considerable. The day after the announcement, the *Daily Herald,* the large local daily newspaper, ran the story, "Crane's District Needs Fresh Face, Challenger Says." [2] The story described Pressl's background and his claim that Phil Crane was out of touch with the district. The piece also outlined some of Pressl's stances on the issues and included a picture of Pressl speaking from a podium with the "Lance Pressl for Congress" logo attached to it. A short article in the *Chicago Tribune,* "Business Leader Enters Race to Unseat Crane," also mentioned some of Pressl's policy positions.[3] Other local papers, including the *Pioneer Press Rolling Meadows Review* and the *News Sun,* ran stories about the challenge for Phil Crane's seat in the House of Representatives.

In the national press the announcement was tied to recent problems that Phil Crane was having. The *Washington Post* ran a story that buoyed the spirits of the Pressl campaign. In "Crane Sends China his Kindest 'Retards,'" the *Post* declared, "Yesterday was not what would be called a great news day for veteran Rep. Philip M. Crane, R-Ill.. Seems Crane, at a gathering with some reporters on the Hill Wednesday, said the Chinese have been "retards"

Representative Crane, pictured here with colleagues David Dreier, R-Calif. (left), and Tom DeLay, R-Texas (right), speaking after the House of Representatives passed legislation that normalized trade relations with China. Crane was taken to task by a Washington reporter for his insensitive comments about the Chinese and their trade practices during debate on this legislation.

on trade matters. This just two days after Washington and Beijing signed a big trade deal that may lead to China's entry into the World Trade Organization next year." [4] The story continued to discuss Crane's insult of the Chinese, indicating that Representative Crane later apologized. The conclusion of the story reported Pressl's announcement and noted that he might appeal to crossover voters. That is, Republican voters who tend to be ideologically moderate might be drawn to vote for a centrist Democrat rather than a Republican candidate who could be portrayed as an extremist. In general, crossover voters are less committed to their partisanship and more likely to support a candidate from the other party if that candidate more accurately reflects their views and issue stances.[5] Clearly Pressl was hoping that any crossover voters in the Eighth District would be attracted to his candidacy, and he expected newer residents in the district to fit into that category.

All things considered, Lance thought, the public announcement of his candidacy had gone well, particularly given all the things that could have gone wrong. The press covered the story and there was no public criticism of Lance's speech at Rolling Meadows High. He began to feel a bit more like a candidate now that he had gone public about his intent to challenge Crane. He was in the race.

The last two months of that year were geared toward establishing a more formal campaign organization. Jane began to look for office space. Lance began meeting with local officials, seeking endorsements from various groups, and working on a set of coherent issue statements so that he could readily answer questions in any forum. He spent hours researching votes that Phil Crane had cast in Congress and on the issues that he himself believed were most important in the upcoming election. Lance paid particular attention to the issues that were most important to him—Social Security, gun control, education, and health care—and was ready to contrast his own views with those of Crane. (Later, Lance would also study the issue stands of both presidential candidates, George W. Bush and Al Gore, so that he could present his own views relative to theirs and allow the voters to view his candidacy in a broader context.) Lance also filled out numerous issue surveys for the interest groups from whom he was seeking endorsements. Typically, all of the major interest groups will send to candidates questionnaires that seek to capture the candidate's views or positions on issues of concern to the group. For instance, the Sierra Club will question the candidate's stands on environmental issues, whereas the National Rifle Association will ask about views on gun control, and so on. The candidates get dozens of these issue surveys and the groups will base their endorsements, in part, on the responses that the candidates supply. This is one of the more important early interactions that a candidate will have with a group. And, of course, there was always the need to raise money.

Lance's closest counsel during this period was his older brother, Larry. They spoke daily, and Larry, a financial planner, provided considerable help with some of the position papers, particularly those that might tap economic issues. Larry also worked very closely with many of the local unions as some of his professional responsibilities involved economic and finance issues related to their pension packages. As a result of the contacts Larry had with the unions, he was able to help Lance in seeking meetings with some union officials as well as some endorsements.

The first "Pressl for Congress" fund-raiser was held on December 7, 1999. Kevork Derdeian, a member of the Chicago Civic Federation Board, hosted the event at Faces—a 1970s disco theme restaurant in Chicago. The invitation to the fund-raiser, which was sent to several hundred people, featured a picture from the Rolling Meadows High School yearbook. Lance Pressl, sixteen years old, was shaking hands with the then-forty-three-year-old representative, Phil Crane. Above the photo the invitation read, "25 Years Ago, Lance Pressl Decided What He Wanted To Do When He Grew Up . . ." Under the photo was the bold statement: "BEAT PHIL CRANE!" The fund-raiser targeted members of the Civic Federation Board and friends of the Civic Federation. It was the first time the new candidate was asking people for money.

The people invited to Faces on this night for an elaborate spread of cheeses and other hors d'oeuvres did not live in the Eighth Congressional District. It is not uncommon for congressional candidates to raise or attempt to raise money from sources outside the district, as like-minded people or groups are frequently willing to contribute to the candidate they think will carry their views forward in Congress. But unfortunately, Lance could not play on the "you deserve better representation than Phil Crane has given you" theme in his remarks to the guests. At this event, Pressl was looking for dollars, not votes, so he tailored his remarks in an attempt to make the guests feel as though they should care about this particular congressional election. Care enough, in fact, to spend their money on it. Pressl's strategy was to remind this audience that his opponent, a longtime member of the House of Representatives, was expected to become the next chairperson of the House Ways and Means Committee. Ways and Means is one of the most powerful committees in Congress because it has jurisdiction over tax issues. Committee chairs are always held by the majority party in the House, and going into the 2000 election, the Republicans had a slim majority. The system for becoming a committee chair is based in part on seniority. The House Republicans have a three-term maximum for chairmanships. Then the position rotates, typically to the next most senior Republican on the committee. Rarely is there a challenge for the position from any other Republican member. Phil Crane was next in line, on the basis of seniority. If the Republicans held on to their majority in the House when the 107th Congress convened after the 2000 elections, many expected that Phil Crane would chair the Ways and Means Committee. And if he did, it could safely be assumed that no new tax dollars would be forthcoming for the arts, education, or any of the other domestic programs that the guests at this fund-raiser might value. Crane consistently opposed federal spending in these areas. Pressl wanted to remind this audience that Crane was the political antithesis of what this group was all about. Because Lance felt self-conscious about promoting himself, he couched his remarks in a tone that suggested, "I understand you may not want to support me, but certainly you want to support Phil Crane's opponent." He focused on Crane's negative qualities, but didn't offer much that was positive about his own candidacy.

Pressl's first fund-raiser took in $10,000. It was not, by any account, a smashing success. The room was "gargantuan," and food had been prepared for one hundred people; only thirty showed up. Some of the guests told their host, Kevork Derdeian, that Lance had not made it at all clear why people should vote for him rather than Crane. "All he did," they grumbled, "was talk about how bad the other guy is." Pressl knew, too, that the evening had not gone very well. "Even one of our friends, who had done some design work, was horribly negative about everything," Lance reported to a friend later. "He was disgusted that no one had nametags. He didn't like the way I was introduced. He didn't like my remarks. He didn't like anything."

All his life, Pressl had been a success. He was used to being praised for doing things well. He wasn't accustomed to being criticized, to feeling like a failure. Asking people for money, people that he knew, had not been easy. And not many of these people had responded with either encouraging words, or money. But Pressl learned a number of important lessons that night. Chief among them was to say something positive at every turn.

The second fund-raiser, held the following week in December, went a bit more smoothly. For one thing, the setting was stunning. Mr. and Mrs. Jack Guthman, a couple well known in the Chicago arts community,

WHEN POWER LEADS MAN TOWARD ARROGANCE, POETRY REMINDS HIM OF HIS LIMITATIONS. WHEN POWER NARROWS THE AREAS OF CONCERN, POETRY REMINDS HIM OF THE RICHNESS AND DIVERSITY OF HIS EXISTENCE. WHEN POWER CORRUPTS, POETRY CLEANSES, FOR ART ESTABLISHES THE BASIC HUMAN TRUTHS WHICH MUST SERVE AS THE TOUCHSTONE OF OUR JUDGMENT.

John F. Kennedy

(Interior)

Dear Lance:

_____ Yes, I will join you at the Guthman's on December 13. We need a strong advocate for the arts in Congress. I want to help elect you by contributing:

_____ $2,000*   _____ $1,000   _____ $500   _____ Other

_____ No, I cannot join you at the Guthman's on December 13, but I am committed to the arts and humanities and want to help elect you by contributing:

_____ $2,000*   _____ $1,000   _____ $500   _____ Other

Please make checks payable to: **Pressl For Congress.**

Federal law requires political committees to use their best effort to report the occupation and the name of employer of each individual whose contributions aggregate in excess of $200.

Full Name:

Address:

City:

Home Phone:

Employer:

Occupation:

E-mail Address:

*The maximum an individual may contribute is $1,000 per election ($1,000 primary $1,000 general). Qualified PACs may contribute $5,000. Non-qualified PACs may contribute $1,000. Federal law prohibits corporate contributions. Contributions are not tax deductible as charitable contributions for federal income tax purposes.

Paid for by Pressl For Congress.
A copy of our report is, or will be, available for purchase from The Federal Election Commission.

Pressl For Congress
P.O. Box 8813
Rolling Meadows, Illinois 60008

Invitation to the fund-raiser held at Jack and Sandy Guthman's home in December 1999. This fund-raiser went more smoothly than did Pressl's first fund-raiser a week earlier. The quotation from President Kennedy is illustrative of two things. First, Kennedy inspired Lance and is central to Pressl's early memories about politics. Second, the Pressl campaign made a conscious effort to emphasize youthfulness, doubtless epitomized by Kennedy's style.

hosted the event in their home. The Guthmans live in a renovated syna-gogue in the Water Tower area of Chicago—one of the most affluent neighborhoods in the country—that is starkly contemporary and open and serves as a showcase for their extensive collection of modern art.

About fifty guests, drawn from Lance and Martha's connections to the arts community and from a mailing list provided by the Chicago cultural societies, enjoyed appetizers and finger foods served by tuxedoed waiters. A bartender busily mixed drinks in the corner of the living room. Even though it was cold outside, the warm feelings of the holiday season were beginning to set in. Jack Guthman's flattering introduction of the candi-date helped ease some of Lance's anxiety, and, having learned from the mistakes of his first fund-raiser speech, Lance's remarks went well. As he concluded, a well-known attorney with considerable campaign experi-ence called out from the crowd "Hey Lance, introduce your mother." After introducing his mother, Virginia, and his wife, Lance once again thanked the guests for coming. As people began to leave, the attorney came up to Lance and insisted, "You always introduce your mother in a campaign, Lance! People like mothers."

This fund-raiser at the Guthman home brought in about $13,000. The fact that this was a friendly crowd of well-to-do people and Lance man-aged to bring in a mere $3,000 dollars more than his first fund-raiser shows just how difficult the fund-raising game is. Moreover, the fact that this was happening within a few weeks of Christmas, a time when people might be expected to be in a giving spirit, made the evening's financial take even more disappointing. But, at this point, perhaps even more im-portant than the money was the boost in confidence that Lance felt when it was over. He was feeling more and more like a candidate. Lance was es-pecially pleased that a prominent figure in the African American commu-nity had attended the event. A successful entrepreneur and member of the Northwestern University Board of Regents, this man was so well thought of that his appearance added to the legitimacy of the event and to the Pressl candidacy. He visited with several of the guests, listened to Lance's remarks, and wrote a check for $500 before he left.

Meanwhile, Representative Crane was enjoying a very different situa-tion. If you are an officeholder, incumbency is a beautiful thing. While some prospective opponent is chasing after dollars, you can be comfortably and routinely doing the job you were elected to do. You might simply send an occasional newsletter to your constituents and remind them that *you* are in Washington doing the people's business. Phil Crane was not going to face any meaningful primary election opposition and, given his long record of electoral success, he had little reason to focus on a young Democratic underdog challenger. The typical incumbent would not think about any real active campaigning until the summer months of the election year, which was indeed when Representative Crane's campaign would become visible.

So, at this time, Crane was pursuing his principal legislative interest, foreign trade, as Lance was in the early stages of the campaign. The stark contrast of a representative presenting worldly legislative proposals while a challenger tries to raise money and launch a campaign is something that experienced legislators love to note in their campaigns. One of the fundamental benefits of being in the incumbent's position is the ability to run on your record and your accomplishments. Challengers run on promises, and they are hardly as easy to sell.

As the calendar changed to 2000, the country was focused on the new millennium and the upcoming presidential election. The Pressl team was looking ahead as well. On January 15, 2000, the "Pressl for Congress" campaign moved into a ground floor suite of offices at 120 West Golf Road in Shaumburg, a sprawling suburb near Rolling Meadows in the heart of the Eighth District. The building was a modern three-story glass structure located next to a car dealership and across the street from a strip mall. The suite, which rented for $1,000 a month, had an outer reception area and five offices—two inner offices, three outer offices with windows. The campaign signed a one-year lease. The rooms were fairly shabby, with ugly wallpaper, holes in the plaster, and carpeting that needed a thorough cleaning. But Lance was thrilled to have a real office and address for the campaign headquarters. He and Martha spent evenings and weekends stripping the wallpaper, repairing the holes in the walls, and cleaning the floors. They wore layers of sweatshirts so they could keep the thermostat on low and save money on heat. Lance bought $600 worth of furniture from a used office furniture warehouse and two additional desks for $50

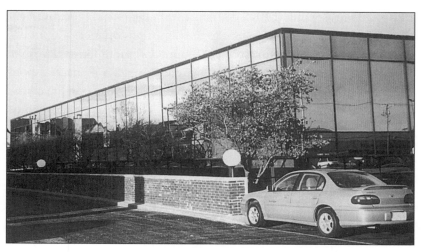

An exterior view of the Golf Road office building that housed the "Pressl for Congress" headquarters. The office space was cold and bare when first rented in January 2000 but would become a bustling hub as the campaign moved along.

from a friend whose office was moving. He purchased several refurbished computers, some multiline phones and other office equipment, and set up shop. One of the inner offices served as a supply room; it housed the copy machine, fax, and a couple of computers. An outer office at one end of the suite was Jane's. She was now on salary—a full-time campaign manager. Next to her was an office for a yet-to-be hired field operations director. The largest of the three outer offices was outfitted as a conference room—a place to hold meetings, eat takeout lunches and dinners— and included a place for Lance to work when he wasn't out campaigning.

Setting up the office was exciting, but always there was the task of raising money. A third fund-raiser was held in February—this time in Washington, D.C. It was hosted by Clare Cotton, President of the Association of Independent Colleges and Universities of Massachusetts. Clare was also the candidate's father-in-law. Though Lance was running to represent the Eighth District of Illinois in Congress, every congressional race has some national implications. Over the years, Phil Crane had not been kind to legislative initiatives designed to provide government support to higher education. Some of Mr. Cotton's professional associates were interested in hastening Crane's departure from the House of Representatives. On this night, $7,000 leapt into the campaign coffers.

Jane Thomas was beginning to feel more and more like a campaign staffer. She attended an intensive course for campaign managers sponsored by the Democratic National Committee. Participants in the course simulated a campaign and were kept working in excess of eighteen hours a day. Jane was the oldest person in her group and, more than once, wondered what she was doing there. She made it through, felt the better for it, and prepared herself for the long, arduous campaign days ahead. She and Lance also began to learn about the campaign industry. They were approached by many campaign professionals looking to sell their services to "Pressl for Congress." All sorts of sophisticated plans and technology were offered, some of which were interesting and all of which were expensive. The hard-sell approach they typically used was disconcerting to Lance. The campaign industry seemed to be all about winning elections, and not a bit about what you stand for or what you are trying to do. Pressl found this demoralizing and wondered if he would even want to hire anyone to run all of the sophisticated campaign software. It was equally sobering to wonder how he was going to pay a political professional, because he knew that, in the end, he was going to have to hire someone who knew how the elections game was played.

In mid-January Lance did hire a political professional. For a fee of $10,000 a month, David Fako and his young assistant Brandon Hurlbut went to work on the "Pressl for Congress" campaign. The choice of Fako was not without political strategy. Fako was described as "Mike Madigan's person" and Mike Madigan was the Democratic Party chairperson in Illinois as well as the powerful Speaker of the state House of Representatives. Lance hoped that by hooking up with Fako he might get volunteer and financial support from the state Democrats. Actually, Lance also spoke to the firm of Penn and Schoen in Washington, D.C., which had done polling work for President Clinton and with whom Lance had worked during his Philip Morris days. He wondered if the national Democratic Party might take him more seriously if he was on Penn and Schoen's client roster, but thought they were too expensive for the risk of being noticed. That is, Lance reasoned that if he went with this more expensive firm and it did not get him noticed by the party powers in Washington, it would have been money poorly spent. In the end, he chose to go with Fako.

Brandon Hurlbut was in charge of setting up a field operation. He carefully analyzed past voting patterns in every town and neighborhood in the district. This allowed him to pinpoint the areas where Pressl should concentrate his efforts. Some areas, for example, would be bombarded with "get out the vote messages," while others would be targeted for repeated visits from Pressl. Fako did not work out of the campaign headquarters. He had other clients to work for and other campaigns to advise. He did, however, speak to Jane on a daily basis, and he kept in touch with Lance via email and in periodic meetings. Under Fako's direction the campaign had a road map to follow. Fako told them what the campaign should be doing and when and how they should do it.

One of the first things that Fako and Hurlbut did was to conduct a public opinion survey of the Eighth Congressional District. The survey was conducted in February 2000 and the results brought some good news for the Pressl campaign. Survey responses showed a fairly high negative rating of Phil Crane. While voters in the district seemed to know who Representative Crane was, they did not view him in a particularly warm or positive way. But the results also showed that Lance was virtually unknown. He had to become much more familiar to the voters in the district and make it clear to them that he offered a viable alternative to Crane.

The poll results reinforced what Lance already knew. His instincts had told him that Crane was out of touch with the voters in the district, that he was not a "beloved" representative. And all Lance had to do was to look around the cold and empty suburban suite of offices that served as campaign headquarters to remind himself that nobody out there in the district knew who he was. In his mind's eye he pictured a bustling campaign office, people coming and going, phones ringing, general hubbub and occasional chaos—all the sights and sounds of political campaigns as Hollywood portrays them. He pictured himself with sleeves rolled up, answering calls, running off to meetings, conducting strategy sessions long into the night. Instead, the phones were often eerily quiet, save for the times Jane or Lance picked up the receiver to make yet another round of calls to ask for support, or to try to set up a meeting with an interest

I'm going to read you brief descriptions of candidates for the U.S. Congress. Once I read the descriptions please tell me which candidate you prefer.

Candidate A is a Democratic challenger who is the president of a civic organization that monitors and keeps the public informed of the government's use of tax dollars. He is a fiscal conservative and social moderate who will work to protect your tax dollars and is pro-choice on the issue of abortion. He supports strong gun control measures. He pledges to be an advocate for all citizens in his district. He will make health care reform, education, and government accountability his priority. His opponents say he is a tax-and-spend liberal Democrat who is not in touch with the values of the district and is not the reformer he claims to be since he once served as a lobbyist for major tobacco companies.

Candidate B is a conservative Republican who has served in Congress for thirty years. He is strongly pro-life on the issue of abortion. Because of his experience and seniority, he is next in line to become chairman of the influential and powerful Ways and Means Committee. His top priorities are tax cuts and cutting government spending. His opponents argue that his opposition to all gun control, support of the NRA, and opposition to meaningful health care reform is extremist and out of line with his district and that he is a status quo politician who has accomplished very little in recent years.

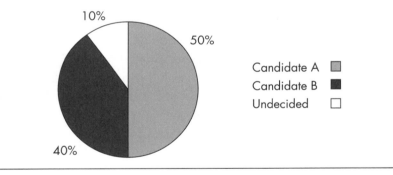

This is a sample from the survey that consultant David Fako conducted early in the campaign. These kinds of polling results (see pie chart)—showing that the thirty-year incumbent was not running away with the campaign—gave the Pressl team hope as the campaign was catching steam. Fako's findings are typical of the kinds of data that campaign consultants produce for candidates. Other surveys tap respondents' issue preferences and overall interest in politics and the specific election, respondents' likelihood to vote, and any other matter that might help the candidate.

group leader, or to line up a speaking engagement. The campaign was only slowly beginning to attract volunteers, and, since announcement day three months earlier, press coverage had been next to nothing.

Things would change on primary day, March 21, 2000.

Lance had put out a press release the day before the election, indicating where he would be voting and what time he would be going to the polls. Absolutely nobody paid any attention to it. He arrived at Carl Sandburg School, where he had gone to junior high, at 9:00 a.m. He gave his name to the polling official, and asked for a Democratic primary ballot. The elderly woman working at the polls did not recognize Lance's name and said, with a mixture of scorn and disbelief, "You mean a Republican ballot, don't you?"

Lance looked down the long hallway where the voting booths had been set up. There were six booths for the Republican primary, two for the Democratic contest. It was a stark reminder of just how Republican the district was. "No," Lance said, "I would like to vote in the Democratic primary." The woman put down her doughnut, sighed disapprovingly, and handed Lance a ballot. Some beginning.

Lance and Martha were the fifth and sixth Democrats to vote in their precinct that day. Even though he was running unopposed, Lance was concerned about being embarrassed in the primary. He knew some people were going to vote for him, but feared that he might receive such a pathetically low vote total that it would be difficult to claim that he was a viable candidate in the general election. He was uneasy all day. There was a plan for a primary election night victory party at the "Pressl for Congress" headquarters that evening; Lance hoped there would be something to celebrate.

What a difference a few hours can make. At 2:30 in the afternoon, Lance got a phone call at home from a local reporter asking for his response to Phil Crane's announcement. Pressl replied, "With all due respect, I don't know what announcement you're talking about."

"Crane announced that he was an alcoholic and that he was checking himself into a rehab center," the reporter told Lance.

"I'm not surprised," Pressl said, "and I wish him the best. My differences with Phil Crane are policy differences, not personal differences, and I wish him well."

Lance quickly made a series of phone calls—to Martha, Jane, his brother Larry, and a few others whose advice he had been seeking throughout the campaign. He then showered, dressed, and headed for the office. The adrenaline was flowing.

For several months Lance had told himself that Crane was going to screw up at some point. He just wasn't sure if *this* was the screwup he had been waiting for. But he did know that this was an important opportunity, and he also knew that he had to be careful how he handled it. He recognized that the announcement could work to Crane's benefit. It could bring out a sympathy vote. Or it might cause people to say, "Look, Phil Crane is taking care of his problem. We should support him."

The primary election night victory party was much more energized than Lance or Jane had anticipated. Crane's announcement was big news in the Chicago media, and reporters from radio, print, and television all wanted a statement from Pressl. Many of Lance's friends, supporters, and those few volunteers who had signed on to the campaign filled the offices of campaign headquarters. Fox Television sent a news crew with a remote camera to videotape a statement from Lance for their 9:00 p.m. news program. The phone was ringing constantly with calls from people offering congratulations. While Lance was giving his statement to Fox, the local ABC station called and said it wanted a statement from the candidate about Crane's announcement and the upcoming campaign for the 10:00 p.m. news broadcast. And so it went, fairly long into the night. People coming and going, supporters and staffers celebrating the campaign's success. Lance tried to savor the noise, the tumult, and the chaos—everything that he had pictured campaign headquarters on election night should be.

Both Lance and Jane thought the media was a bit relentless in their efforts to get the campaign to say something inflammatory about Crane. It was clear that reporters would have loved a "He doesn't deserve to be in Congress" response to the announcement that Phil Crane was seeking treatment for his alcoholism. Lance was careful to keep pointing out that while he differed with Crane in terms of political philosophy and their stances on the issues, he felt no personal ill will toward Crane. When pressed by one reporter, Lance simply said, "I wish the congressman and his family well in what is obviously a difficult time for them."

The end of that March primary election day could hardly have been more different than the beginning. Lance had started the day unrecognized as the Democratic candidate when he went to the polls to vote. He ended the day as part of the lead story on the evening news. The crowd and the noise and the celebration in his office breathed life into the campaign, and he truly felt like he was in the race for Congress. He knew, in fact, that until primary election night, there really had been no campaign. "Now," he said to himself, "it really is Pressl versus Crane in the Illinois Eighth." The real fight had begun.

Notes

1. Paul S. Herrnson, *Playing Hardball: Campaigning for the U.S. Congress* (Upper Saddle, N.J.: Prentice-Hall, 2001), 3.

2. Jon Davis, "Crane's District Needs Fresh Face, Challenger Says," *Daily Herald,* November 18, 1999.

3. "Business Leader Enters Race to Unseat Crane," *Chicago Tribune,* November 18, 1999.

4. Al Kamen, "Crane Sends China His Kindest 'Retards,'" *Washington Post,* November 19, 1999.

5. The usage of the term *crossover voter* by the *Washington Post* should not be confused with the concept of "crossover voting," which refers to the primary election strategy of members of a particular party voting in the opposing party's primary in an effort to produce weak opposition. The *Post* instead refers to Republicans who might be swayed to vote for Pressl. *Crossover voters* is a common journalistic term for voters who defect from their own party to the opposition in a particular election.

In the Office and on the Trail
Managing Resources

THE PRIMARY VICTORY and the election night media coverage energized the Pressl campaign. Lance and his campaign manager, Jane Thomas, finally felt like they were legitimately in the race, and they began putting themselves on track for the head-to-head competition with Crane. In the spring the office became a busier place. Dave Fako continued to touch base with Jane each week, giving her guidance about what she and the rest of the campaign staff should be doing. Brandon Hurlbut, Fako's young assistant, moved into an office at campaign headquarters and began in earnest to direct the field operation.

Having Brandon in the office on a daily basis gave a boost to the campaign. He was able to take over some of the tasks that Jane had been juggling, and his previous experience in electoral politics made him a valuable sounding board for both Lance and Jane. Armed with an undergraduate degree in political science from the University of Illinois, Brandon Hurlbut was a character straight out of central casting. He was in his early twenties, slight in build, chewed gum constantly, and spoke in a very quick staccato. He appeared to be always in motion—even when he was sitting at his desk. The Pressl campaign was not his first job in electoral politics, and it wasn't going to be his last. He planned on a bright future in political consulting.

Before signing up with Lance, Brandon had been with the Bill Bradley campaign. He had worked to get Bradley's name on the Democratic presidential primary ballot in Illinois and then went to Iowa to help Bradley in that state's influential party caucuses. He operated with a confident "let's get to work" attitude in the precincts that were giving the Bradley forces the most trouble. When Bradley's effort to win the Democratic presidential nomination ended early in 2000, Brandon went to work for Fako and Associates, a political consulting firm. Through Fako, Brandon had come to work on the "Pressl for Congress" campaign.

Brandon brought an earnestness and enthusiasm that was most welcome in Pressl's office. He was in regular contact with other Democratic campaign organizations in the area and was always looking for new ways to promote the Pressl candidacy. No undertaking was too great, and no task was beneath him. Whether it was helping with a press release or tacking "Pressl for Congress" signs to wooden stakes to be carried along a parade route, Brandon took on the job with gusto.

Brandon's primary responsibility, however, was to run the campaign's field operation. This involved, among other things, using data gathered from the state Democratic Party and the local board of elections to analyze the district's electoral patterns. In particular, he focused on the votes cast in every precinct in the previous congressional election. Then he categorized voters in the Eighth Congressional District as hard-core Democrats, hard-core Republicans, or "persuadables," in order to figure out exactly where the Pressl campaign should focus its resources.

Brandon's handiwork was evident whenever Pressl's daily schedule included "walk time." During walk time Lance and Brandon campaigned door-to-door in areas of the district where Brandon believed that a personal visit by the candidate would translate into votes. Brandon, clipboard in hand, carried voting records of the precinct they were visiting. Typically dressed in khaki trousers and a white golf shirt with the blue and red "Pressl for Congress" logo emblazoned over the left breast, Lance carried a small stack of campaign literature. If no one came to the door, he left a brochure. If someone answered the knock or the doorbell, Lance gave an upbeat greeting "Hi. I'm Lance Pressl and I'm running for Congress from this district. I just wanted to stop by to say hello, ask you to look at the material that talks about my candidacy, and ask for your support in the November election."

On occasion, these short visits would give Lance and Brandon real hope. Their spirits were buoyed when people responded with "Good, I hope you win. You can count on my vote. That Phil Crane has been there much too long and doesn't do anything for us." Brandon or Lance would then quickly suggest that word of the Pressl challenge be shared with friends and neighbors. But there were far too many moments when Lance was told that a "young fella like you don't stand a chance against Phil Crane. He's been there forever." Comments like that made humid afternoons even more unbearable, and the sweat-soaked "Pressl for Congress" shirts clung even more uncomfortably to the skin.

"Walk time" also produced some very funny moments. There was the time, for example, when Lance and Brandon approached a woman who was walking from her townhouse to her car. Lance, brochure in hand, greeted her. "Hi, I'm Lance Pressl and I'm . . ."

Before he could finish the woman waved him off. "Listen here," she said, "I ain't buyin' no magazines, candy, Kool-Aid, raffle tickets or any other shit you be sellin'. " Pressl chuckled sympathetically. "I'm not selling anything. I'm running for Congress and I'd just like to give you this brochure."

Without missing a beat, the woman responded, "I ain't buyin' that either." Brandon looked at Lance and shrugged. "I guess she's not a persuadable."

Brandon quickly became a valued member of the Pressl campaign staff. Finding someone to raise money proved to be more problematic. Fund raising produces "the lifeblood of campaigning." [1] As Lance was acutely aware, without money there are no staff members, no yard signs, no bumper stickers, no ads—nothing to bring visibility to the campaign or the candidate. Initially, Pressl employed the services of a fund-raising consultant, Amy Szarek, who had been successful in raising money for Democratic candidates in Chicago. Lance hoped that she would bring the same kind of fund-raising prowess to his campaign. Unfortunately, Amy wasn't able to transfer her successes in heavily Democratic Chicago to a congressional district dominated by Republican voters. After a short stay, Amy left the Pressl campaign, and Kim Rogers was brought on board to organize and handle fund-raising activities.

Kim was taking some time off from her undergraduate studies to do political work during the 2000 campaign season. She had worked for

Ralph Nader, gathering signatures to get him on the ballot in Illinois for his presidential bid. And, like Brandon, she had worked for Bill Bradley's presidential campaign in Iowa. Kim and Brandon had enjoyed working together, and as so often happens during campaigns, the two young staffers had become more than just friends. Brandon recommended Kim to Lance, and she was hired to keep the campaign finances in order.

One of Kim's tasks was to help prepare the various reports that candidates must submit to the Federal Election Commission. All congressional candidates are required by federal law to file disclosure reports that indicate how much money was raised during the reporting period, the sources of that money, how it was spent, and the amount of cash that a campaign has on hand. Kim

Kim Rogers of the "Pressl for Congress" staff. In her early twenties, Kim had considerable campaign experience for her age. She joined the Pressl campaign in the late spring of 2000 and, in addition to working on the campaign's finances, was always ready to do any task asked of her. In this photo Kim is preparing to pass out "Pressl for Congress" literature at one of the many parades in which the Pressl team participated.

worked on these reports and also assisted in fund-raising for the campaign. When a fund-raising event was scheduled, Kim helped with everything from ordering food to preparing nametags, and she often greeted the guests as they arrived. She also helped with another fund-raising activity—"call time."

A finance director's equivalent to the "walk time" that directors of field operations schedule is known in the campaign business as "call time." The candidate, in a closed-door office, sits with the finance director and makes calls to solicit potential donors for financial contributions to the campaign. The early list of donors for the Pressl campaign was drawn from Lance's personal contacts. Initial calls to family, friends, and business associates elicited additional potential donors. Amy Szarek, Lance's first finance director, also had provided a list of names from her professional contacts. While Lance was never entirely comfortable asking family members and friends for financial help, it was certainly easier than making "cold calls" to complete strangers whose names appeared on lists constructed by various members of the campaign staff.

"Call time" goes something like this: After a brief conversation about current events or the campaign, the candidate gets around to asking for money. If the finance director thinks that the call is going too long, he or she holds up a sign saying "GO FOR THE ASK," which lets the candidate know there's been enough small talk. It's time to ask for the money and move along. Like many candidates, Lance was not fond of this part of campaigning. Kim, on the other hand, took on "call time" with a competitive spirit and actually enjoyed the process, even though she was often put in the position of forcing the candidate to do something he didn't want to do.

The importance of money cannot be overstated, particularly the importance of money to an underdog candidate challenging a longtime incumbent for a seat in the House of Representatives. The incumbent begins the race with a large advantage in name recognition, and the strategic use of the perquisites of the office continues to make the incumbent well known to the voters. It takes hundreds of thousands of dollars for the challenger to gain enough visibility to compete effectively, and for any candidate lacking in personal wealth, raising money is absolutely critical. This suggests that an adequate amount of cash only allows the challenger to attempt to level the field against the incumbent. This is particularly difficult given that, on average, incumbents can usually outspend challengers by a margin of nearly three to one. For every thousand dollars a challenger is able to raise and spend, an incumbent has three thousand.[2] It should also be noted that it is the candidate himself who is most important in raising money. People making donations want to develop a bond with the candidate or the officeholder—not an underling.[3] So, not only was getting contributions critical for Lance, it was something that he could not delegate. His voice needed to be the one potential donors heard on the other end of the line.

As spring turned into summer, there was a certain rhythm to the days at campaign headquarters. But things were far from perfect. As the pressure of the challenge grew more intense, and as work demands increased, tension among the staffers began to surface. For one thing, key members of the campaign organization disagreed about the performance of David Fako. Jane Thomas, the campaign manager, was happy with Fako. She spoke with him every morning by telephone, and on many days spoke with him several other times as well. They also stayed in regular contact via email. Jane viewed Fako as a pro and valued his advice. She thought of him as an integral part of the campaign operation who was working very hard on behalf of Lance.

Indeed, Dave Fako was a pro. And as a political professional, he expected a candidate to devote every waking hour to getting elected. Winning was paramount; politics was a business and the bottom line of the business was winning. Neither ideology nor a candidate's positions on the issues were very important. Jane could accept the fact that that was how Fako operated, and she saw him as an asset to the campaign.

Pressl, on the other hand, was finding it increasingly difficult to deal with David Fako. The candidate believed that Fako should be providing a more detailed, concrete, long-term plan for the campaign. Never particularly fond of Fako's style, Lance grew increasingly resentful that Fako wanted to schedule his every waking hour. If Lance was not in the office calling around for money, Fako thought he should be out meeting voters. Even personal time should be scheduled—and it should come after the responsibilities one assumes as a candidate. More than once Fako said to Lance, "If you have to spend time with your wife, put it in the schedule." And Jane knew that when, in the course of her conversations with Fako, he asked to speak with Lance, the political professional would blow a gasket if she reported that Lance was out on his daily jog. So, to protect Lance and to minimize the tension that was building between the candidate and his campaign consultant, Jane usually said that Lance was at a meeting. Fako, dissatisfied, typically countered with "Who in hell is he meeting with?" All Jane could do is tell Fako that Lance would call him later.

It's not uncommon for candidates and their consultants to have a clash of perspectives. Campaign professionals are about winning. They are hired for their expertise, and they want to make sure the person paying the bill runs as well as possible.[4] Victories also make consultants more valuable to other candidates who may hire them in the future. People running for office, on the other hand, try to balance their issue positions and, in some cases, their ideals, against going all out in the name of winning. And they can become easily frustrated with professional consultants if the campaign seems to be floundering. Thus it's not unusual to have abrupt shakeups in campaign personnel or changes in the direction of a campaign. Just as the manager is often fired if the baseball team is doing poorly, the tenure of a campaign consultant is often short lived if the candidate is unhappy with the campaign being waged.

In June, Lance severed his relationship with David Fako and made other changes to the campaign staff. At this point Pressl was balancing his academic training, which inclined him toward a thoughtful, even ponderous posture that called for careful consideration of every conceivable option, with his desire to move swiftly and wage a strong, effective, and ultimately winning campaign. He knew that he was not going to do well running on his party label, as Democrats had always run poorly in the district. He also knew, at least intellectually, and this too was reinforced by his training as a political scientist, that there is not much of a relationship between candidates' positions on issues and how people vote. Research has consistently shown that issues are not terribly important in congressional campaigns. But candidate *appeal* seems to be of increasing significance as politics become more candidate centered and less party centered. Indeed, Lance was working hard to be viewed as an appealing, capable candidate. This, of course, as he played it out, kept him positive about his own message, and kept him away from going negative about Phil Crane.

During this period, Brandon Hurlbut received a job offer from Dorothy Brown, the Democratic candidate who was running for election as clerk of the Circuit Court in Chicago. Certain to win, Brown told Brandon that he would have a paid position on her staff after the election, and that he could also go to law school while working for her. While Brandon admired Lance a great deal and shared Lance's views on the issues, the future with Lance was more than a little uncertain. Lance hated to lose Brandon but understood why the young man felt he should leave the Pressl campaign.

Even though Brandon was gone, the campaign still had a sense of vitality. More volunteers started coming to the offices of "Pressl for Congress." Chief among the volunteers were Ann and Martin Ryan. Ann was a retired nurse and Martin had retired from the deanship at the college where Jane had taught. They were at virtually every campaign activity, and Ann spent a lot of time in the headquarters office as well. They and the other volunteers took on much of the thankless work that goes into running a campaign—answering phones, stuffing envelopes, and making endless rounds of calls to ask for help in the effort to defeat Phil Crane. These volunteers represented a cross-section of what Pressl thought would be the coalition that would sweep him to victory in November. There were people whose primary interest was in the arts, and those from the world of higher education. There were young parents concerned about safety in schools and members of the gay and transsexual communities. There were volunteers representing the small African American community in the district and volunteers from the growing Latino population. And there were hard-core Democrats who felt they finally had a chance to defeat Phil Crane.

The Crane campaign was still relatively invisible in the early summer. Crane returned to work after the rehab treatment and stayed out of the press and the limelight. He was, however, very active in the Congressional Republican Caucus as he sought to gain support for his bid for the chairmanship of Ways and Means, a position he still very much wanted should he win reelection and the Republicans retain control of the House. It is not at all uncommon for an incumbent of Crane's longevity to not be campaigning very actively at this early stage. Most incumbents, in a presidential election year, will wait until after the national nominating conventions, which typically take place in July, and are sometimes scheduled for as late as early August, to begin getting involved in the campaign. And typically, unless the incumbent feels very threatened by an opponent, he or she does not really become visible until after the Labor Day holiday.

During the summer there was no shortage of events for Pressl to attend. Festivals, street fairs, block parties, and outdoor art fairs took place all over the district. In addition, Lance was invited to fund-raisers for other candidates, and he went to as many as he could. One such fund-raiser, held for a candidate running for county commissioner, took place at the local multipurpose entertainment facility in Round Lake, a small town in the woodsy countryside northwest of Chicago that is home to a growing number of Latino citizens. Part bowling alley, part game arcade, part miniature golf course, part restaurant/bar, the place was filled with the sounds of neighbors and friends sharing stories, discussing politics, and telling the children to play a little more quietly.

Lance was greeted almost like a visiting celebrity. He had spent a fair amount of time with the local mayor, Ila Bauer, a spirited middle-aged woman who was popular with her constituents because she was willing to address community problems with practical solutions. One of her most interesting and successful innovations had been the establishment of a truancy court. Local magistrates presided over cases involving young people who had stopped going to school. Parents and siblings were required to come to the court along with the truant student when the case was heard. Sometimes, in the course of the hearing, it became clear that a student might have missed school in order to care for younger siblings while their parents worked at nearby farms. The family was then told about child-care programs and other family support services. The benefits of education were discussed, and expectations for student behavior were laid out. Thus the truancy court served an additional purpose of socializing new citizens into the community and encouraging their productivity. Lance admired Ila and appreciated her concern for the people in her area who were struggling to "make it" in a new country.

Amid the noise of the bar, the bowling, the arcade games, and the music, donations were taken and raffle tickets sold to support the campaign of the local candidate. Lance spoke to the guests, indicating how important these grassroots efforts were to bring good people into office. As supporters stood around drinking beer from plastic cups and eating chips and guacamole on a hot summer night, they nodded their agreement, donated their money, and pledged to continue working through the fall election season.

The evening in Round Lake was a far cry from the sophisticated Chicago fund-raiser that had been held for Lance during the winter holiday season. Lance was genuinely interested in the issues relevant to this working-class community. On a more practical level he knew that his involvement in these sorts of very local, party-oriented events was an important part of what he had to do to win in November. The largely Latino population that made up this community were among the very people who were not being served by Phil Crane, and they were a large part of the reason Lance was in the race. Finally, there was a genuineness about the crowd there that evening, their obvious warmth for one another, and the joy that they took in their children, who were having fun running around making noise, that made the event very satisfying and had the effect of making Lance feel good about his decision to challenge Crane. The Eighth Congressional District was a mix of densely populated suburbs and more rural areas, and as he drove from place to place, Lance often reflected on the different kinds of people he would represent in Congress. His travels throughout the area were a constant reminder that the demographics of the district had changed considerably during the course of Phil Crane's tenure in Congress, and Pressl knew that he needed to put together an electoral coalition that included people from all walks of life.

Summertime in Illinois is parade season. It seems as though every town has a parade as part of a festival or celebration. Independence Day, of course, is a particularly big day for parades. On Saturday, July 1, the Jaycees hosted the annual Independence Day parade in Palatine. Bordering the wealthier communities of Barrington and Inverness, Palatine was one of the largest towns in the district. The area was heavily Republican, and Phil Crane had always carried it by large margins. In recent years, however, Palatine had become home to a significant number of working-class families who had moved into a host of newly constructed apartment complexes. Lance did not expect to do very well in Palatine, but he believed that because of the influx of new residents he had a chance to do better than previous Democrats. The parade route was likely to be lined with the

Rep. Phil Crane is driven to the staging area for participation in a parade. By the Fourth of July, 2000, the Pressl team believed it had managed to worry the incumbent enough to spur him to return to the district for parades that he had not been part of for years. Because incumbents are typically so heavily favored, challengers are always pleased to hear that they might be getting under an incumbent's skin.

moms and dads of Little Leaguers and Girl Scouts, and Lance decided it couldn't hurt to make some connection with these young families.

Jane and Lance learned just two days before the parade that Phil Crane's staff had asked parade organizers to include a spot in the parade for the representative. It was the first time in anyone's memory that Crane had come home for the parade in Palatine. The Pressl campaign was elated. They heard from a number of people that Crane was showing up because he was starting to get nervous about the Pressl challenge.

Before the parade, guests and VIPs gathered at a local bank for a continental breakfast. Lance and Martha saw a few familiar faces, but Lance felt a bit like a fish out of water in this solidly Republican town. One woman, a member of the school board, engaged Lance in an animated discussion about education. She told him that she liked many of his views on early childhood education and wished him well in the campaign. As she walked away, Lance overheard her say to another guest, "He's a bright young guy. Too bad he doesn't stand a chance."

After a few more minutes of "meeting and greeting," the president of the Jaycees thanked the breakfast sponsors and indulged in the usual self-congratulations to his Jaycees for all of their good work. "Give yourselves a hand," he encouraged the crowd. Then it was out into the muggy sunshine and the staging area where the parade participants lined up to travel the parade route.

The "Pressl for Congress" group gathered around a shiny Chrysler convertible that belonged to one of Jane's sons. A number of Pressl supporters gathered to march in the parade. Kim Rogers was there with Brandon Hurlbut, who had rejoined the Pressl team for the day to participate in the parade. Jane was at the wheel of the car. There were also several volunteers, including some of Lance's friends from high school and their young children; a friend from the African American community; and the retired community college dean and his nurse wife who seemed to be at every Pressl event. The volunteers were all wearing "Pressl for Congress" T-shirts and were prepared to carry campaign placards or hand out literature as they walked the two-mile parade route. The volunteers and staff joked with one another and drank bottled water from the cooler in the backseat of the convertible while they waited for nearly an hour to begin walking in the parade in their assigned spot.

As they pulled into position to join the parade, the Pressl people had quite a bit to smile about. They sensed that they had gotten under Phil Crane's skin and brought him out to a parade he didn't want to be in. And they had come to this Independence Day event buoyed by several recent newspaper articles that had brought good press and much-needed visibility to their candidate.[5] Steve Neal's "Talking Politics" column in the *Chicago Sun-Times,* for example, had posed the question: "How can we miss Crane if he won't go away?" The column noted that while Phil Crane had once been a strong advocate of limiting U.S. senators and representatives to six-year tenures, he was now in his thirty-first year as a member of Congress and was seeking reelection to another term. Neal went on to suggest that in more than three decades in office, Crane had yet to define himself. "Crane," Neal wrote, "who has never been renowned for his work ethic, has accomplished little during his long tenure. He has also fallen out of touch with his constituency." Lightly regarded even by his

Republican colleagues on Capitol Hill, "Crane is facing a credible Democratic rival in Lance Pressl," Neal concluded.

That same week, the *Daily Herald* ran an article describing Pressl's challenge to debate Phil Crane in "33 Lincoln-Douglas-style exchanges designed to reach every voter in the district." And two days later, a piece in the *News Sun* reported that the Illinois AFL-CIO had endorsed Pressl in his bid to win the congressional seat for the Eighth District. The article quoted the president of the Illinois AFL-CIO: "Phil Crane has been in Washington D.C. too long, blatantly ignoring the needs of working families and is out of touch with the concerns of the families in Illinois' Eighth District. Lance Pressl was born and raised in the community, he is in touch with the values of the families of the Eighth District and he has the energy and commitment to get the job done."

These are uncharacteristically tough words to be hurled at a longtime representative, and certainly most incumbents do not suffer this kind of invective. In fact, the job of the legislator is a very demanding one, with most of the hard work done well outside the glare of the spotlight. Moreover, we might imagine the Crane people reading the AFL-CIO endorsement and scoffing, "If we're so out of touch, why do we keep winning?"

The Pressl team knew that most people are not as interested in politics, let alone as passionate, as a state AFL-CIO president. And although the endorsement used tough words, they were coming from a group who had opposed Phil Crane for thirty years. Lance could only hope they would stir up some interest in other voters who might not be connected to an interest group or political party. It was those voters who were previously disinterested, or new to the district, or more moderate than Crane on social issues that Lance had to reach.

So, as the Independence Day parade in Palatine began, the "Pressl for Congress" campaign felt that it was finally getting noticed. The streets of the parade route were lined with children and their families sitting in lawn chairs or on the curbsides in the pleasant residential community. The fire department and the police department blew their sirens and flashed their lights. There were floats of all kinds sponsored by community groups and local soccer teams and the Little League. As they wound their way along the parade route, riders on the floats threw candy to the children sitting along the sides of the streets. From a flatbed pulled by a diesel rig, officials from a truckers' union passed out key rings. The driver periodically blasted his air horn, adding to the din.

Pressl's contingent had been placed directly in front of a marching mariachi band—perfect for calling attention to the candidate. Some staffers and volunteers carried large "Pressl for Congress" signs as they walked in front of and behind the car that Jane was driving. Other Pressl supporters walked along each side of the parade route handing out campaign brochures and putting "Pressl for Congress" stickers on all the children they passed. The children loved the stickers; many of them ended up with several adorning their shirts and caps. Lance ran back and forth across the street to shake hands and to greet voters on either side of the parade route.

The Pressl team, all decked out in white T-shirts with "Pressl for Congress" emblazoned in blue and red, exuded energy and enthusiasm. They were rewarded with warm and friendly greetings from the crowd. Some people marveled at Pressl's stamina as he ran back and forth across the street shaking hands. One balding fellow in a sleeveless T-shirt and plaid Bermuda shorts put down his can of Budweiser and called out from his lawn chair, getting Pressl's name wrong, "I'm voting for this guy Presswell. Look at him running back and forth like he gives a damn. The other guy, Crane, just sat on his ass in the car." Some people along the parade route began chanting "Lance, Lance, Lance," and a few young women screeched, "He's sooo handsome!"

Lance met old friends and made new ones during the Independence Day parade in Palatine. People stepped out of the crowd to tell Lance they remembered him from high school and to ask how they could help with his campaign. He was hugged by women he hadn't seen since they were all teenagers; some asked how they could get in touch with the campaign to volunteer. At one point along the way Martha heard Lance muse, "Gee, I didn't know I had so many old girlfriends."

When the parade was over the Pressl brigade sought shade under a tree and relaxed with bottles of water and soft drinks. A few people walked up to ask if there was a place for them in the volunteer corps. One man pulled no punches as he introduced himself. "Hi, Lance. I hate Phil Crane, and I really want to help you."

Lance chuckled and replied, "Thanks. We can really use your help. I think we can beat him."

"You bet we can," the man agreed. Lance learned that his new acquaintance was a software engineer at Motorola. He had grown up in Chicago, was in his early forties, and was raising his family in Rolling Meadows. He viewed Crane as woefully "out of touch."

"Phil Crane," he told Lance, "has been in Congress for thirty years, and he wields no significant power after all that time. He is worrying about trade while we are all worrying about education and school safety. Even if I wasn't a lifelong Democrat, I believe I would say that it is time to retire Phil Crane. Here's my business card. Call me and let me know what I can do to help."

Lance shoved the card into his pocket and turned to find Martha. He was hot and tired, but he couldn't stop smiling. It had been an invigorating day on the campaign trail. It certainly felt like a campaign, with all the noise and activity Lance had pictured on those cold nights six months earlier when it was just him and Martha, painting and patching walls in an empty office. Indeed, he was in the thick of it, he believed that his candidacy was being noticed, and he knew that he was facing all the typical ups and downs of running for office. There was the constant fund-raising need, the staffing shake-ups, and a heavy dose of uncertainty. There were also moments of quiet satisfaction and unbridled exhilaration. The days were long, and there was no shortage of things to do, but he was glad to be where he was, and eager to keep going.

At this point Lance was consumed by the campaign. He had also started to take on a number of psychological characteristics common to most candidates. Research shows that at some point every candidate begins to believe that he or she is going to win. This happens because candidates tend to focus more on the positive feedback they receive from voters and actually filter out responses that suggest things may not be going well. One political scientist captured this when, after his own unsuccessful run in a congressional primary, he wrote of politicians' "incredible ability to delude themselves about their own chances." [6] Similarly, in an early study of candidates running for office, John Kingdon found that a "congratulation-rationalization" effect seemed to be present.[7] Kingdon's study suggested that candidates who win elections tend to congratulate themselves for the fine job they did in running for office and also congratulate voters for the fine choice that they made when casting their ballots. The loser, on the other hand, rationalizes the loss by suggesting that the voters didn't pay enough attention and perhaps were not competent in how they judged the issues, or some variety of other factors that were beyond the loser's control. The "reality" of the situation is probably somewhere in between.

Though Lance was undergoing the important process of making the psychological leap to candidacy, there were other possibly more objective factors that would come into play. One recent study of challengers to congressional incumbents suggests that the quality—and hence viability—of a candidate may be determined by considering two different types of characteristics. The first is strategic qualities, which include things like name recognition, fund-raising ability, party support, interest group support, and one's own ability to fund a campaign. The second are personal qualities, and they include integrity, problem-solving ability, ability to work with others, public speaking skills, and a grasp of the issues. The findings of the study indicate that, perhaps surprisingly, personal wealth is far less important than other characteristics when defining a quality candidate, and that personal qualities such as a desire to serve the public, integrity, issue awareness, and communication skills might be considered more important traits in determining a quality challenger.[8] Not surprisingly, incumbent members of Congress were found to have a considerable advantage over challengers where strategic qualities are concerned.

So, given that strategic qualities are actually *less* important than the personal qualities, the Pressl campaign would have found the study's findings very heartening. Without question, Lance scores much higher on the personal quality factors than on the strategic quality characteristics. He had an orientation toward public service, was a student of contemporary issues, presented himself well, and was perceived as a person of integrity. Thus, if the race were to be run on personal qualities alone, the Pressl campaign would have reason to believe that they stood a reasonable chance of winning.

Elections, however, don't play out in such ideal environments. It is foolhardy to exclude the strategic qualities noted above. In those respects—party support, funding and fund-raising capability, name recognition, and interest group support—we know that the incumbent has an extraordinary advantage. So while the Pressl people may have thought, particularly in the excitement of an Independence Day parade, that their chances were pretty good, they could certainly have been better.

How do challengers get around these hurdles? Some studies show that those who are in a position to overcome the name recognition advantage of incumbent members of Congress are well-known public figures who have attained great notoriety in other public arenas. That fact is driven home by the electoral success of astronauts, sports figures, and entertainers. Certainly, Tom Osborne, the beloved head football coach of the University of Nebraska Cornhuskers, did not have a name recognition problem in 2000 when he ran as a Republican for the open Third District House seat in Nebraska. Osborne had absolutely no political experience, but he still was elected with about 80 percent of the vote. Sen. Jim Bunning, R.-Ky., served in the House of Representatives prior to his successful Senate campaign. Before serving in the House, Senator Bunning had an all-star major league baseball career that saw him pitch no-hit, no-run games in the American League for the Detroit Tigers and in the National League for the Philadelphia Phillies. Rep. Steve Largent, R-Okla., had a record-setting career as a receiver in the National Football League with the Seattle Seahawks, and former New Jersey senator Bill Bradley was a basketball star with the New York Knicks. From the entertainment world, Fred Grandy served in Congress from his home state of Iowa after playing the role of Gofer on the popular 1970s and 1980s television series, *The Love Boat;* and Sonny Bono joined the House of Representatives from California after a very successful recording and television career as half of the duo Sonny and Cher. Because Lance Pressl did not compare in public notoriety to these figures, he was going to have to do a lot of work to overcome the name recognition problem that most congressional challengers have.

None of this was necessarily on the minds of Lance Pressl or his campaign staff. They did not have time to think about academic studies or celebrity politicians. The summer would be packed with a variety of campaign activities: street festivals, more parades, meet and greets, lots of handshaking, and a lot of time in the hot midwestern summer sun. There were also surprises ahead that none of them could possibly anticipate.

Notes

1. Paul S. Herrnson, *Playing Hardball: Campaigning for the U.S. Congress* (Upper Saddle River, N.J.: Prentice-Hall, 2001), 75.

2. Ibid., 216.

3. Frank I. Luntz, *Candidates, Consultants, and Campaigns* (New York: Basil Blackwell Inc., 1988), 27.

4. Herrnson, *Playing Hardball,* 72.

5. Steve Neal, "How Can We Miss Crane If He Won't Go Away?" *Chicago Sun-Times,* June 12, 2000; Chris Fusco, "Pressl Invites Crane to 33 Debate Sessions," *Daily Herald,* June 17, 2000; Election Briefs, "AFL-CIO Backs Pressl in Contest vs. Crane," *News Sun,* June 19, 2000.

6. Roger H. Davidson and Walter J. Oleszek, *Congress and Its Members,* 8th ed. (Washington, D.C.: CQ Press, 2002), 67–68.

7. John W. Kingdon, *Candidates for Office* (New York: Random House, 1966), 146–147.

8. L. Sandy Maisel, Walter J. Stone, and Cherie Maestas, "Quality Challengers to Congressional Incumbents: Can Better Candidates Be Found?" in Herrnson, *Playing Hardball,* 19–20.

5

The Dog Days of Summer
Developing a Campaign Style

THE ENTHUSIASM OF the crowd at Palatine's Independence Day parade buoyed the spirits of Pressl and his team as they hit the summer campaign trail. Lance told his staff that he thought they were making headway, and he hoped he could translate some of the warmth he had felt along that parade route into votes.

There was much to do in July. Because Brandon Hurlbut had decided to leave the Pressl campaign to work for another candidate, Lance needed to fill the position of field director with someone he could trust. He named Pete D'Alessandro to the post. Pete came highly recommended by Kim Rogers, Lance's finance director. Kim had once worked for Pete on a gubernatorial campaign in Iowa, and Pete had brought Kim and Brandon on board the "Bradley for President" campaign earlier in the 2000 electoral season. Both Brandon and Kim told Lance that Pete would be a terrific addition to the Pressl campaign. They were so enthusiastic about Pete's skills that Lance looked no further and offered Pete a spot on the "Pressl for Congress" team. Pete was working as a consultant on a congressional race in Oklahoma and still had some ties to the now-late Paul Wellstone and his Senate office in Minnesota. Pete accepted Lance's offer and joined the campaign.

Pete's first Pressl campaign activity was accompanying Lance to a fund-raiser at Eli's, a famous steak restaurant in the Water Tower area of Chicago. Tom Hynes, a former Cook County assessor and stalwart of local Democratic politics, served as the master of ceremonies for the event. Larry Pressl, Lance's brother, introduced Hynes to the crowd and

The fund-raising event at Eli's restaurant was important to Pressl. A number of key figures in Illinois Democratic politics and the business community attended the event. The participation of so many prominent people boosted the morale of the Pressl team and helped demonstrate the viability of Lance's candidacy. Tom Hynes, former Illinois state senator, Cook County assessor, and member of the Democratic National Committee, pictured here with Lance, is one of the most respected and influential political leaders in Illinois.

said a few warm words about his younger brother. Larry, along with a number of Lance's business and professional contacts, served on the campaign advisory committee. Lance particularly valued his brother's perspectives, especially given Larry's background in finance. With an undergraduate degree in business from Harvard and further study at the prestigious Kellogg School at Northwestern University, Larry had served in a number of banking and finance-related positions. On Lance's campaign, Larry was particularly involved with developing donor lists, providing financial advice, and working to get union support for Lance. The brothers were close and spoke daily during the course of the campaign.

A few days after the event at Eli's, Larry traveled to Jefferson City, Missouri, on business. The next day, July 14, Lance was on a conference call

Lance and Martha greet Woods Bowman at the Eli's fund-raiser. Bowman, a former Illinois state legislator and chief financial officer of Cook County, was active in local Democratic politics. Meeting and greeting is almost endless for candidates, and fund-raisers are critical to getting money—the lifeblood of contemporary politics—into campaign coffers.

with a governor's task force when he was interrupted by an urgent message. Lance's mother, Virginia Pressl, was calling with news that couldn't wait. Larry had been found dead on the bathroom floor of his Jefferson City hotel room. Larry had gone to dinner the night before with a business colleague with whom he was traveling, but didn't answer phone calls or respond to a knock on the door the following morning. The hotel staff had been notified, and they had discovered the body.

Upon hearing the news, Lance went numb. His reactions were fueled more by adrenalin than calculation or clear thinking. He immediately made plans to fly to Jefferson City so that he could identify the body and make arrangements to bring Larry home to Chicago. Almost instinctively, he also made sure that the critical tasks of the campaign were accomplished. Monday was the deadline for filing a quarterly financial report with the Federal Election Commission. Kim and Brandon, who had offered to help out in any way they could, were dispatched to Lance's condominium to pick up his computer and the necessary records to complete the report over the weekend.

On the flight to Missouri everything seemed surreal. Lance's thoughts raced from Larry, to their childhood, to how his parents would cope with this tragedy, to whether he should continue his challenge to Phil Crane. He wasn't at all sure he could concentrate on running an effective campaign or that he had the heart even to try. Larry had died just a few days shy of turning forty-five, and it would be some time before Lance could come to grips with the fact that his only sibling was gone.

On Saturday, back home with his family in Illinois, Lance took a long walk with Larry's twelve-year-old son, Patrick. They talked about the things that Larry and Patrick had liked to do together and about what could have brought on the heart attack that took Larry away from them. At one point Lance asked his nephew what he thought his father would want Lance to do about the campaign. "I think he would want you to win," Patrick said matter-of-factly.

Lance canceled a couple of campaign commitments over that weekend but decided to go ahead with plans to participate in the parade in Lake Zurich, a small town in the northern part of the district, on Sunday. Jane had told him that there were plenty of volunteers to cover the event, but Lance thought it would be easier to go back to the work of campaigning sooner rather than later. He ran the parade route, shaking hands and greeting people, just as he had in all the other parades that summer. For a short while he was able to lose himself in the noise and the tumult of the parade, putting off, if only for a short time, the exhaustion and grief that would be with him for some time to come.

Funeral services for Larry were held Monday, July 17. Lance spent the day with family. The next day Lance and Martha drove to their favorite spot in the Michigan Dunes near the southeast corner of Lake Michigan. Trying to make sense of all that had happened, they talked about Larry, his children, and what the future held in store for the whole family. They also took stock of the future of the campaign—where it was headed and if it should continue. By the end of the evening they agreed that too much of an emotional investment had been made in the campaign and too many people were counting on Lance to finish the race. He had to keep going.

Lance, Virginia, Al, and Larry Pressl in the summer of 2000. This picture was taken just a few weeks before Larry's sudden death. There is no way for a candidate to anticipate the emotional ups and downs that characterize a campaign.

As the month drew to an end, Lance was grappling with the changes that had occurred in his personal and professional lives. The changes in campaign staff were sometimes difficult to deal with. The new field director, Pete D'Alessandro, was very different from Brandon Hurlbut in personality and in work style. Pete was older, more experienced in politics, and a whole lot tougher than Brandon. To Pete, Lance was just another candidate, and this was just another congressional election. While Brandon had been a bit of an idealist and had shared Lance's view of the world, Pete was a pragmatist. He calculated that if Lance did absolutely nothing before election day, he could get about 29 percent of the vote, because about one-third of the district consistently voted Democratic. If Lance were to win the election, it would not be because people were voting for Lance Pressl. Rather, they would be voting against Phil Crane.

As chief strategist, Pete wanted to play up the differences between Pressl and Crane and pound away at what he perceived to be Crane's negatives. A fresh face and a change in representation were not enough; the voters in the Eighth District had to be convinced that the incumbent, Phil

Crane, had not changed as much as the district had over the course of thirty years. The data showed, for example, that a majority of the district's voters, about 60 percent, favored abortion rights. Pete urged Lance to point out at every opportunity that Crane did not. The polling data also indicated that there was considerable concern in the electorate about health care, education, and school safety. Pete wanted Lance to continue to emphasize these issues—and the fact that Crane had paid little attention to them—at every turn. The margin of victory, as far as Pete was concerned, would come from relentless criticism of Crane's ultra- conservative views on domestic social issues. In short, Lance had to go on the attack.

Pete's strategy stood in sharp contrast to one of the initial lessons Lance had learned during the campaign. The feedback from his first fund-raiser had cautioned him against being negative about Crane. Instead, Lance was told, he should be positive about himself. Lance wasn't sure if he could now change his approach to fit Pete's strategy. And he wasn't at all comfortable with Pete's style. Whereas Brandon had been a go-getter who couldn't sit still, it seemed that Pete never got out of his chair. Lance had gotten accustomed to Brandon's staccato, "just-the-facts" way of speaking. Pete, on the other hand, liked to pontificate about any subject imaginable. Even Jane, who was very even-keeled, wondered if Pete could do anything but talk.

There was something else gnawing at Jane about Pete. Jane was a believer. That is, she believed that with enough hard work, Lance could win. She respected the fact that Brandon thought Lance was a long shot, because that did not hamper his willingness to do anything for the cause. Like Jane, Brandon was an optimist. Jane did not get that sense of emotional commitment from Pete. There was something perhaps too clinical about him, something that gave the impression that to Pete, Lance was just another candidate and just another paycheck.

Despite the sadness that now tinged Pressl's personal life and the turnover that had taken place in the campaign office, the candidate managed to keep to the work schedule that had been mapped out earlier. It was difficult, however, for Lance to concentrate on "call time." This task had never been easy for him, and it became even more difficult during the summer. Pete chastised the candidate for not "going for the ask" quickly enough, and Lance grew increasingly irritated when Pete questioned his judgment about when it was appropriate to ask a prospective donor for money. Pete knew, however, that friction between a professional campaign consultant and the candidate was inevitable. Whereas the campaign professional is brought on board to tell the candidate what to do, the candidate is the boss. As Pete observed, "It doesn't take a genius to figure out that there's going to be some friction in any situation in which a subordinate is constantly telling the boss what to do. That's precisely why there's so much turnover in the campaign business. Politics involves a lot of egotistical people trying to tell each other what to do."

Throughout the summer, Lance continued to meet with local officials in an attempt to enlist their support, or even better, gain a public endorsement. Lance wanted local officeholders to know that if elected, he intended to be a presence in the district. One such meeting that took place near the end of July was with Chief Bob Jones of the Gurnee Police Department. The meeting proved to be a primer in the complexities of the relationship between a legislator and his or her constituency. After being ushered into Chief Jones's office, Lance introduced himself as the candidate running against Phil Crane. "Nice to meet you," the chief replied. "You've got your work cut out for you."

Lance settled into his chair and asked the chief, "What are the big issues you're facing in Gurnee?"

"Out here," Chief Jones began, "we police the roadways. I've got a population of 28,000 and another 25 million tourists each year. Those tourists come with a lot of money to visit the Six Flags–Great America amusement park or the huge Gurnee Mills mall. If we ticket too many African Americans, we're accused of racial profiling. If we pull over too many young drivers, we're accused of having it in for the college kids. If a drunk hits somebody, people say we should have had him off the road before the accident. We're in a tough position. And, of course," the chief continued, "the police industry is not perfect. You can't do anything about this, but here's another problem I have. Even when I know I have an officer who should be dismissed, my hands are tied. As soon as I try to fire an officer, I'm in court with the union, and then I'm explaining $100,000 in legal fees to the city council. I don't know how we can reduce the power of the union without closing it down, and that certainly is not an option around here. And I do understand where the union people are coming from. They're just trying to protect their people."

The chief sat back in his chair. "There is one issue that we should talk about," he said. "Gun laws. What are we doing about all the guns that are out there?"

"How about enforcing existing laws and using some common sense?" Pressl offered.

"That's not enough," Chief Jones countered. "People gotta' stand up to the NRA [National Rifle Association]. There's a lack of concern for society at the expense of lobby groups."

Lance suggested that kids also need to be taught respect, and respect has to start at home when children are young. "There is a program," the chief responded, "called 'Fight Crime, Invest in Kids.' There's a chapter here in Illinois. The problem, of course, is how far do you go in telling parents how to raise their children . . ." The chief's voice trailed off, as if he were revisiting all of the frustration of police administration at once.

Pressl jumped into the silence. "Crane is a proponent of the 'conceal and carry' law for firearms."

"I am absolutely dead set against it—and I think the community is against it, too," Chief Jones said. And with that, the chief's full attention was redirected to the conversation with Lance.

"Another issue," Chief Jones said emphatically, "and I alluded to this earlier, is random stops. We need the ability to stop suspicious cars. Why do race and ethnicity always have to become issues? We stop a suspicious car, and suddenly it's a bigger deal than the reason we stopped the car. We know there are increases in heroin use and other designer drugs, but as soon as we stop a car because we suspect drugs, it's a race issue."

Pressl wondered aloud if the media had muddied the waters in this regard. "They certainly haven't been helpful," the chief replied. "I personally don't think that there's anything wrong with taking boats and houses and cars away from drug dealers to wage the war on drugs. But give the TV people just one hint of misbehavior on the part of the police and that's the story they lead with on the evening news. It's complicated. It's not just about drugs, it's also about the violence and the disregard for others that always comes along with the drugs. I guess it goes back to what you said about parental responsibility. But it seems to me, not to sound like Hillary Clinton or anything, it takes a community to raise a kid."

As the meeting was winding down, Lance posed one more question to the chief. "What can I do for you in Washington?" Bob Jones was quick with an answer. "You can work with the Illinois Association of the Police. We need to work through issues without knee-jerk responses. We need to have dialogue."

With that, the meeting was over. Lance thanked Chief Jones for taking the time to see him, and the chief wished Lance luck in the election. As Lance drove back to campaign headquarters, he thought about the conversation he had just had. At one point the chief said that someone needed to stand up to lobby groups like the National Rifle Association for the good of society. At the end of the meeting, Chief Jones told Lance that, if elected, he should work with the Illinois Police Association. Lance mused for a minute about the irony in having the chief say, in essence, "Stand up to lobby groups, but work with my lobby group." Only in the world of politics could such a seeming contradiction pass for logical thinking.

That said, Lance knew that interest groups and the political action committees (PACs) they create are vital cogs in the legislative machinery. Corporations, labor unions, or other organized interests establish PACs for the sole purpose of advancing their political and policy desires. In addition to making financial contributions, PACs develop long-term relationships with legislators that revolve around the policy interests of both the group and the legislator. Presently, there are about four thousand PACs, and no successful candidate or member of Congress can afford not to be cognizant of the role they play.

Lance sought financial support from all of the groups that endorsed him. He had a fairly traditional Democratic constituency in the National Organization for Women; Emily's List, a liberal, grassroots women's group whose name is an acronym for "Early Money Is Like Yeast (it makes dough rise)"; and various labor unions, among others. And they did come through with some money. Police and law enforcement communities, on the other hand, aren't always traditional supporters of Democratic

The Pressl campaign received endorsements from nearly all the major unions in the area. Here Lance is pictured meeting with a member of the Teamsters Union.

candidates, and this makes for an interesting paradox in politics. They are typically union members, a fact that steers them toward the Democrats. Of course, they are also very strong advocates of law and order issues, which makes their agenda compatible with the Republicans'. In meeting with police and fire agencies, Lance wanted to convey that he was moderate enough to work very comfortably with them, and that he intended to keep open lines of communication if he were elected.

Throughout the summer Lance continued to attend fund-raisers and hold meetings with other Democratic candidates in the area. At some events he was lending support, at others he was looking for support. In late July Lance went to an evening fund-raiser for a state senator, Lisa Madigan. The senator's father, Mike Madigan, was the powerful speaker of the Illinois House of Representatives, so most of the movers and shakers among Democrats in the Chicago area were there. This event, like so many others of its kind that Lance had attended, followed a prescribed ritual. The candidate for whom funds were being raised stood in a receiving line of sorts, greeting folks as they arrived. After a few words with the candidate, the guests mingled with one another and helped themselves to food and drink. Most of the conversations were superficial, and everyone appeared to be looking past the person they were speaking with to make sure that they were not missing out on talking to someone more important. The handshaking, the backslapping—it seemed endless. This night Lance was asked often how his race was going and how he was holding up. Many of the guests offered their condolences on the loss of his brother. Pressl kept smiling graciously, thanked his fellow Democrats for their kind words, told them that the campaign was going well, and mentioned that he was looking forward to his own fund-raiser the following month.

On the first night in August, a "Pressl for Congress" fund-raiser was held at an upscale Italian restaurant on the Chicago River. The campaign had high hopes for this event, because the featured guest was Rep. Barney Frank, a gregarious long-term incumbent from Massachusetts. Frank was an openly gay member of the House and something of an icon among political liberals. He was a personal friend of Lance's in-laws and had said he would be glad to help Lance's campaign in any way he could. Pressl's staff scheduled a fund-raiser to coincide with a speaking engagement that Frank had planned in Chicago. Barney Frank was a natural draw for donors from the gay community, and people who worked in the arts saw him as a champion of their causes. These groups were not about to vote for Phil Crane. Pressl hoped that they would lend their much-needed financial support as well as their votes to his effort to unseat the incumbent.

Representative Frank arrived at the fund-raiser from his hotel by taxi. He wore a slightly rumpled dark suit, and his tie was askew. He was completely without pretense and seemed a bit uncomfortable with the fuss that people were making over him. Though there were other officeholders and candidates in the crowd, they hung back. This was Lance's show and Barney Frank was the man of the hour. The other guests were also somewhat subdued and seemed more serious and purposeful than those at the recent Madigan fund-raiser.

Soon after Frank arrived at the restaurant, the evening's host introduced Lance. By now Lance was at ease speaking to a crowd. He mentioned many of the things he had said countless times before—that his district had not been represented by a Democrat since the Civil War, that

The fund-raiser featuring Rep. Barney Frank, D-Mass. (left), was a success. Frank, a popular and long-serving incumbent, added legitimacy to the Pressl campaign. Dorothy Brown is also in this photo supporting her fellow Democratic candidate. Brown, the candidate for Cook County clerk of the Circuit Court, for whom Pressl campaign staffer Brandon Hurlbut went to work, would win her race on election day and become the first African American elected to that office. She was very popular and won by a margin of more than four to one. Lance was grateful for the support of these Democrats.

the world had changed since Phil Crane first came to Congress, that Phil Crane appeared not to have changed at all during his thirty years on Capitol Hill. Lance reiterated the issues that would get him elected—education funding, a woman's right to choose, support for the arts, health care, prescription drug benefits, and protecting Social Security from a privatization plan that was being touted by conservatives like Phil Crane in the 2000 election cycle. Lance thanked the guests for coming and expressed his gratitude to Representative Frank for his support. Then, to the warm applause of the fifty people in the room, Frank stepped forward to speak.

The representative managed to deliver a powerful message without forgoing his trademark sense of humor. He said Lance Pressl was the kind of person that he would like to have as a colleague in the House of

Representatives. Phil Crane, in his opinion, was the most conservative member in the House, and, with the exception of Strom Thurmond, the long-serving senator from South Carolina, Crane was the most conservative person in Congress. Laughing, Representative Frank noted that he wouldn't be able to say that if Dick Cheney, who was about to accept the nomination as the vice presidential candidate of the Republican Party, was still in the House of Representatives.

Frank told the crowd that if the issues Lance had highlighted earlier were important to them, then they must work to defeat Phil Crane. He also talked about campaigning. "It's drudgery," Frank said, " and anybody who tells you that they like this drudgery is either sick, lying, or some kind of psychopath." His audience chuckled appreciatively. "Here you have a citizen," Frank continued, "who is willing to go through the heartache and the exhaustion of a campaign, to leave his job, to try to serve. It is your responsibility to support him. You must support him as much as the legal limit allows financially, and you must contact anyone you know who has any connection to the 'D Triple C' [Democratic Congressional Campaign Committee] and urge the committee to support Lance financially, too. Campaigning is expensive—even more so when you're trying to beat a longtime incumbent. It's very difficult to beat a longtime incumbent, and I can only say that because I'm a thousand miles from home."

Frank was charming as he challenged the folks who had come to the fund-raiser that night. "It probably is the case that Phil Crane is ignoring his district and taking his reelection for granted. As far as I'm concerned, Lance is giving you a 'put up or shut up' election. If you've ever complained about entrenched incumbents, or bad candidates, or lack of a choice, then here is your chance to do something. You have a qualified citizen who has made considerable personal sacrifices to try to represent your interests. If you don't get out there and support him as fully as you possibly can, then as far as I'm concerned, you have forfeited your right to complain about the quality of candidates you get in the future."

Representative Frank finished his remarks with a reminder that control of the House was at stake in this election. "The Democrats only need to pick up a few seats in the 2000 election to regain control of the House of Representatives, and your support of Lance will help make that possible. I believe we can pick up four seats in California alone, and that leaves us needing just a few more. With some help from the top of the ticket, I believe we are in a good position to recapture control of Congress. I don't know what else I can say to impress upon you how important it is that you support this candidate in every way possible."

With the applause for Barney Frank still ringing, Lance again thanked everyone for coming. He invited them to have something to eat and drink and to visit with Frank, who chatted casually with some of the guests. "Do you really think Crane can be beaten?" someone asked.

Frank paused for a moment, and then said quietly, "Yes."

Then he said it again, this time more forcefully. "Yes. And I'll tell you why. There's always one race, in every election cycle, that nobody sees coming. Not the national media, not the party, not the experts. But some grassroots, issue-oriented group manages to elect a candidate in a surprising outcome. This race strikes me that way. I think Phil Crane is ripe to be beaten."

Of course, Representative Frank knew that the odds were against Pressl. Incumbents have the capacity to raise far more money and can do so much more easily than their challengers. That money is spent on campaign activities that ensure the continued name recognition of the incumbent, and name recognition and funds go a long way toward perpetual reelection. It has been demonstrated that Republican incumbents who are not in competitive races can be expected to have about eight times as much money as their challengers, so indeed Frank knew that Pressl was running against a pretty stiff wind.[1] But on occasion challengers do win. It takes a combination of factors that include adequate funds, timing, an incumbent that might be losing touch with his district, and an attractive, aggressive challenger. It also doesn't hurt a challenger to have the good fortune to be facing an incumbent who is warding off a scandal. Finally, successful challengers are usually adept at blaming their incumbent opposition for "the mess in Washington." [2]

The evening with Barney Frank was an unqualified success. The event raised $15,000 for the campaign, and it was reassuring for Lance and his staff to spend some time with people who believed in his candidacy. It was also gratifying to have a seasoned professional like Barney Frank offer support and say positive things about Pressl's effort to defeat Crane. Throughout August the campaign tried to hold on to Representative Frank's encouraging words as day after day they knocked on doors, met with local officials, spoke to any group or club that Jane could get the candidate in front of, and called potential donors. Pete believed that if they could raise $300,000 in the three months before the election, the staff could put together several targeted mailings as well as some radio commercials that would give them a serious shot at upsetting Phil Crane.

As the Pressl team was holding its fund-raiser with Barney Frank, the Republican National Convention that would nominate the presidential–vice presidential ticket of George W. Bush and Dick Cheney was being held in Philadelphia. The contrast between the glamour and glitter of the nationally televised Republican convention and life on the campaign trail in Illinois' Eighth Congressional District was stark. The Crane campaign had not geared up yet and really was not expected to until well after the convention. Crane attended the convention, and the *Daily Herald* reported that this was Crane's first appearance at a national convention since 1980, the year that he ran for president. The trip to the convention was in part to further his bid to become Ways and Means Committee chair.[3]

The piece in the *Daily Herald* did provoke some letters to the editor, many of which took Crane to task for what they saw as his token appearance. Two letters in particular were hard on Crane:

To the Editor:

I was more than a bit surprised to learn that Phil Crane has not attended a Republican national convention in 20 years ("Crane Makes Rare Visit to a Convention in His Bid for Committee Post" Aug. 3).

Given his well-documented penchant for paid junkets, I would have thought this would have been a slam-dunk for him. If he hasn't been going to these conventions, where has he been?

If you believe his rhetoric, he is supposed to be the "conservative conscience" of the Republican party. Wouldn't you expect him to be guiding the party and demonstrating a leadership role in drafting the party's platform?

Wouldn't you expect, given his 30 years in Congress, that he would be offering sage advice to every Republican presidential hopeful since 1969? Doesn't he owe it to the party and the voters who put him in office?

The sad and troubling answer is that Phil Crane has been shunned and ignored by his own party. How else can you explain his absence for 20 years?

If there has ever been a wake-up call that it is time to elect someone new, the time is now. On Nov. 7, I am going to vote against Phil Crane and do something I rarely do. I'm going to vote for the Democrat, Lance Pressl, running against him.

Even if I don't agree with Pressl 100% of the time, at least I will have a better chance that he will show up at important meetings and do what he can to represent his constituents.

I would rather have action than inaction any day.

M. O.
Schaumburg[4]

The second letter read:

To the Editor:

So Congressman Crane has not attended a Republican National Convention since 1980. ("Crane Makes Rare Visit to a Convention . . ." Aug. 3)

What a surprise considering that Crane has one of the poorest attendance records in the House of Representatives, seldom attends subcommittee hearings, and in general seldom participates in almost all political functions.

He never participates in open debate on the House floor and is never seen on television supporting his Republican colleagues and/or openly discussing his views with others on any major issue.

Now he wants to become active again so he can be selected as chairman of the House Ways and Means committee.

It seems to be a bit late to become visible and active after 30 years of representing this district virtually in absentia.

A. P.
Palatine[5]

Although Pressl and his staff certainly were glad to see their sense of Crane's performance corroborated by a few Republican voters who had previously supported the incumbent, they knew quite well that they were the underdog in a long uphill battle and that Phil Crane would be back to campaign, just as he had been every second autumn for nearly the last three decades.

When the calendar turned from August to September, the big push began. A generation ago, politicians thought of Labor Day as the beginning of the "official" campaign season. After the events of Labor Day weekend, candidates would take a short break for planning and then shift into high gear after the World Series ended in late September. As the baseball season began to stretch into October, however, politics could no longer wait for the summer game to end. Now, Labor Day merely marks the point in the electoral season when the candidates must start to run flat out.

"Pressl for Congress" had a large contingent on hand to participate in the Schaumburg Labor Day Parade. This was due, in part, to the efforts of Mike Poleski, a young man who had worked for Pete in Iowa and who had recently joined the Pressl staff. Mike was put in charge of grassroots mobilizing, which meant that he was responsible for recruiting volunteers and managing their efforts on behalf of the campaign. Families with small children in strollers, Latinos, members of the gay and lesbian community, senior citizens, African Americans—all were carrying "Pressl" placards and wearing "Pressl for Congress" T-shirts despite the gray day and the cold, misty weather. The parade was slow to start, and participants were held in a staging area for nearly an hour and a half before starting along the route. On cue, when the parade finally began, the light rain stopped and the sun peeked through the clouds.

With so many summer parades and festivals under their belts, the Pressl campaign knew just what to do and what to expect. Lance would run along behind the group, crossing the street from side to side, greeting voters and shaking hands. The people in front of Lance's vehicle would carry "Pressl for Congress" signs that featured a large picture of Lance. Onlookers would ask, "Where's Lance? Where's Lance?"

The volunteers in the front of the Pressl group would answer, "He'll be along, he's shaking hands. He'll be along."

"In retrospect," Lance's wife, Martha, said months after the election, "by the end of the campaign, we really had the parade thing down."

In this Labor Day parade Lance rode along on the back of a flatbed truck, jumping off to shake hands and jumping back on as the truck rounded corners or drove past those places on the parade route that didn't accommodate onlookers. As the parade wound its way down the streets of Schaumburg, Lance was thrilled with the reception he was getting. People were literally screaming his name and grabbing at him to get his attention and to shake his hand. His large, diverse group of supporters and his own youth and energy were making a statement. It couldn't have been going any better.

Then disaster struck.

The next thing Lance knew, he was on the ground. He thought he felt someone stepping on the back of his foot. Then he heard something snap, and he couldn't walk. He looked up and thought he saw two strangers quickly walking away from him. These strangers might well have been the foggy perception of a man on the ground writhing in pain, and a likely scenario is that a campaign staffer and Lance both jumped off the flatbed at the same moment and their trajectories intersected, causing Lance to get stepped on. In the end, Lance wasn't sure what had happened, but he did know that he was in a great deal of pain. He was also angry, frustrated, and bewildered. Would he ever catch a break?

Lance had fallen just as he was passing the parade's reviewing stand. The mayor of Schaumburg had seen Lance go down, and he left his seat to get a golf cart to move Lance off the street. Before the mayor could reach Lance, a police officer wearing a 1920s-style uniform and driving a three-wheel motorcycle in the parade picked Lance up and drove him to the end of the parade route. The police officer waited with Lance until Martha and Lance's mother could bring a car around to take him to the nearest hospital emergency room.

Lance was not a bit surprised when the emergency room physician reported the results of the x-rays. His Achilles tendon was completely torn, and surgery was necessary to repair the damage. Given his pain and the demands of the campaign, Lance wanted to schedule the surgery immediately. But this was a holiday weekend, and surgery would have to wait. He was told that he could call the hospital in the morning and schedule surgery for later in the week. Lance left the emergency room tired and dispirited. Wincing in pain, he wondered what else could possibly go wrong.

Barney Frank had said at the beginning of the month that campaigning was "drudgery"—for Lance, it had just become very painful drudgery. The underdog position of challenging a longtime congressional incumbent has been well documented, and Pressl knew what he was getting himself into when he decided over a year earlier to undertake the campaign. He knew that like all challengers, he would have a hard time raising money, and he knew that the odds were against him. He did not, however, have any way to prepare for losing his brother and then his physical mobility, too, in the height of the campaign season.

Notes

1. Paul S. Herrnson, *Congressional Elections: Campaigning at Home and in Washington,* 3d ed. (Washington, D.C.: CQ Press, 2000), 153.

2. For a good discussion of nonincumbents who do win, see Roger Davidson and Walter Oleszek, *Congress and Its Members,* 8th ed. (Washington, D.C.: CQ Press, 2002), 112.

3. John Patterson, "Crane Makes Rare Visit to Convention in His Bid for Committee Post," *Daily Herald,* August 3, 2000.

4. M. O., "Crane's Inaction," Letter to the Editor, *Daily Herald,* August 17, 2000.

5. A. P., "A Little Late Now," Letter to the Editor, *Daily Herald,* August 16, 2000.

6

Race to the Finish
Campaign Dynamics

ON SEPTEMBER 6, 2000, two days after the accident, the *Chicago Tribune* ran a small blurb about Lance's injury. "Parade Leaves Politician Paying Painful Price," the headline read:

> In Chicago, politics is the No. 1 spectator sport. But, a contact sport too?
>
> Just ask congressional candidate Lance Pressl, who is undergoing surgery Wednesday after his appearance in a Labor Day parade in Schaumburg.
>
> Democrat Pressl, who is trying to unseat veteran conservative Republican U.S. Rep. Phil Crane in the 8th Congressional District, was cheerfully marching in the Monday parade, shaking hands.
>
> That's when disaster struck. "I turned to sprint across the parade route to shake hands on the other side of the street," Pressl told INC., "when someone stepped on the back of my heel—this as all of my energy was propelling me forward. My Achilles tendon just split in half."
>
> . . . He says he will be campaigning on crutches for two weeks and then in a walking splint for another month or so.[1]

After his surgery Lance greeted Martha in the recovery room with a grin. "Wow, I slept so well," he said. "I can't remember the last time I slept so soundly."

As soon as Lance was released from the hospital, Martha drove him straight to campaign headquarters. There was a long-scheduled meeting with the Harper Community College faculty that afternoon, and Lance felt he had to attend. Not wanting to be perceived as some kind of "bad luck kid" who was going to give up, Lance needed to send a message, not only to the faculty members but also to his own staff and closest support-ers. He wanted everyone to know that being on crutches was simply a small setback, and that it was not going to affect his participation in the campaign. On the way to the meeting Lance thought about something that had happened at the parade, just after he had fallen and was waiting to be driven to the hospital. A campaign volunteer had come over to him and said, "I know you're probably in a lot of pain now, but could you just come over and shake hands with my son? He marched with me in the pa-rade for you and would really like to meet you, but he's a little too shy to come over here."

"Absolutely," Lance had replied.

"There was no way I wasn't going to shake that little boy's hand, " Lance told Martha as they got closer to the office. "But wow, did it ever hurt to move."

Martha nodded her head in agreement. "You did the right thing," she said as she pulled the car into the parking lot. "A lot of people have in-vested a lot of time in your candidacy. They're counting on you. You can't stop now. You've got to continue to run hard in this race . . . even though you can't walk," she finished with a grin.

As Lance was learning how to maneuver on crutches and getting used to having his mother drive him to all of his appointments, Jane Thomas was dealing with yet another problem with the campaign personnel. As she was scheduling Lance's time, trying to arrange speaking engagements, put together coffees, direct the volunteers who were coming and going to help get out fund-raising mailings, she felt that the campaign lacked the sort of razor sharp edge and concrete get-out-the-vote plan that only an experienced political operative could provide. Simply stated, the office was not running smoothly, she was trying to do too many things, and the campaign lacked focus.

Since Brandon Hurlbut's departure, things in the office had suffered. Kim Rogers, the person in charge of finance, had left the Pressl campaign in August. A young woman named Molly Ray had taken over fund rais-ing, and Jennifer Pohl had been hired to do press work. Jennifer was fresh out of college and eager to work, hoping to make up for her lack of experience with energy. Pete D'Alessandro, the loquacious professional, simply was not delivering, and Jane was feeling like an adult supervisor in a college fraternity house.

Pete was frequently in Minnesota, consulting with another campaign, and when he was at Pressl headquarters he was either on the phone or on the computer—quite often playing fantasy baseball or other computer games. It also seemed as though every time Jane pressured Pete on where some particular project was, Pete would say, "I 'lateralled' that to Mike." Mike Poleski, the young staff member that Pete brought to the campaign did not begin to have the experience or know-how to do the job. Jane just could not shake the feeling that the Pressl campaign was not a priority for Pete, and that this was affecting Mike's work as well.

With Lance's blessing, Jane met with Pete one Monday morning to voice her concerns. She told Pete that the office had fallen into complete disarray, and that the campaign needed a full-time field director. Pete could tell from the tone of the meeting that it was time to focus on the other races he was involved with and leave the Pressl campaign. He also knew that politics was not a business in which one ever burns bridges, and he offered a suggestion that would prove very helpful.

At the end of their meeting Pete told Jane that Claude Walker, a very well-regarded field director, was back from the Pacific Northwest. Did Jane want Pete to call Claude about working for Lance? Jane was glad to hear that Claude might be available. The Pressl campaign had hoped to hire Claude at the same time Pete joined the staff. His name had been floated by a number of Lance's contacts as someone who had a great deal of experience with campaigns in general and press relations in particular. But Claude had just been called to work on a campaign in Washington state and could not join Lance earlier in the campaign season.

"If Claude is going to accomplish what we need to have done around here, by all means, call him," Jane told Pete.

By Thursday of that same week, Claude had moved into Pete's former office and Jane was back to overseeing the day-to-day operation of the campaign. Claude was forty-eight years old and had spent his adult life in politics and government since graduating from Loyola University in 1974. He had worked for Common Cause, a citizen lobby in Washington, D.C., and then helped open the Chicago office of that organization in the late 1970s. From Common Cause it was on to more grassroots work for the Citizens Utility Board (CUB) in Chicago and then to Pat Quinn's successful campaign for state treasurer in Illinois. Claude remained to work for Quinn for a few years and then began hiring himself out as an independent campaign consultant. He was experienced in both field operations and media relations. He had also worked with some of the big-name Chicago Democrats on their campaigns, including all of the late Harold Washington's successful mayoral campaigns in Chicago. He had most recently been in Washington state working on a bruising Democratic primary campaign for a U.S. Senate seat.

Claude was confident and willing to work. He quietly went about putting everybody in the office back on task. He set an example by working hard to develop a campaign plan for the final weeks before the election. Jane was relieved to have a real "pro" at the office full-time, putting the pieces together and moving the campaign forward.

As September unfolded into October and Lance was able to trade his crutches for a walking splint, the pace of the campaign became more frenetic. The days began early. Lance stood at busy suburban train stations, shaking hands and passing out literature. "Call time" followed the morning rush hour. Then Lance met with any group that would have him. Unions, Kiwanis, Lions Club, local chambers of commerce, Jaycees, Knights of Columbus—Lance was glad to speak to any organization that opened the door to him. It was extremely difficult to arrange speaking engagements, as is typically the case for a Democratic challenger in a heavily Republican district. (The same would be true of a Republican challenger in a heavily Democratic district.) Jane had set up a database that contained every civic, community, professional, senior, and ethnic organization that she could identify in the district and spent endless time on the phone trying to line up opportunities for Lance to speak. The weekly Pressl email to volunteers also contained a plea that if any of them belonged to organizations where Lance might speak, or even be introduced, to please let Jane know. A campaign manager that Jane had met during her training suggested that Lance crash meetings and just start introducing himself, but the fear that this "in your face" approach might generate more negative than positive reaction caused them to reject that idea. Also, Jane said, that really was not Lance's style.

Lance (center) with teamsters on the picket line on a blustery spring day. Lance knew that he needed support from the unions, and he took seriously the responsibility to return that support. He was always glad to meet with any group that would have him, and the unions are crucial to the success of any Democratic candidate in the Chicago area.

Friends and acquaintances also hosted "coffees" in their homes and invited a few friends to meet the candidate. These were informal gatherings. Typically, Lance spoke briefly, answered questions, and asked people for their help and their votes. The back end of his Ford Explorer was always loaded with yard signs for people to take home with them and put up on their front lawns. If any of the guests knew of stretches along public thoroughfares that would be good places for signs, volunteers were dispatched the next day to put the signs in the ground. Jane also attended these coffees and always brought preprinted forms to collect names, phone numbers, and email addresses of anyone who might work on the campaign as a volunteer as election day approached. She also had volunteer information cards, contribution cards, and campaign literature in adequate supply to be used as needed.

The constant struggle for money weighed heavily on the campaign. Lance would have liked to begin the targeted mailings at this point, but

Friends and acquaintances hosted coffees as opportunities for the candidate to meet with voters informally. Lance is pictured here at one such event. These small events were important for drafting volunteers and getting the campaign's message out to interested citizens. Ann Ryan, a loyal and hardworking campaign volunteer, coordinated the events for Lance.

that would have to wait until closer to election day, given the campaign's budget. Claude and Lance also began putting together the scripts that would air on the radio closer to the election. Certainly they were all putting in long hours.

The Crane campaign was still quite silent in October. But opposition to the Pressl campaign became more visible: the following story from the *Chicago Tribune* suggests that Representative Crane still had active support in the district.

Political Pilferer Fails to Tear Down Sign Owner's Spirit

There's nothing new about the perfidious purloining of political yard signs. But Oak Park's TQ White II didn't take it kindly when the 4-by-8 foot plywood Al Gore sign he made for his front lawn was swiped and torched in an alley near his house. He repaired the huge sign and hooked it up to a motion detector that rings a security alarm in his house if anyone touches it. He's had no problems since he brought in the heavy artillery. Not so lucky Northwest suburban Democratic congressional candidate Lance Pressl, running against incumbent Republican Phil Crane, said thieves made off with the yard signs from the block where Pressl grew up in Rolling Meadows—including the dozen or so on the lawn of his folks, Al and Virginia Pressl. Pressl tells INC. one of his neighbors made a sign that said, "My Pressl for Congress sign was stolen but Give Lance a Chance." Um, that sign was stolen too . . ." [2]

On October 16 the rhythm of a typical week was altered somewhat by a big event for the Pressl campaign. Phil Crane had agreed to accept an invitation from the AARP to debate Lance in a morning session at the Round Lake Area Park District Community Center. In sponsoring the debate, the AARP/VOTE project sought to provide a nonpartisan voter education program about issues of concern to senior citizens. Pressl would certainly have preferred a time that was accessible to more voters, and a less rural location, but as an underdog challenging an entrenched incumbent, he was glad for any chance to debate Crane.

The moderator for the session was David Beery, the editorial page editor of the *Daily Herald*. The panel of questioners included John Herman, a representative from AARP, Lucia Jones, a representative from the Northeastern Illinois Area Agency on Aging, and Robin Kilbane-McFadden, vice president of the League of Women Voters of Lake County. Coffee and doughnuts were set up on tables along the side of the room. A crowd of about 125 people sat on folding chairs, and there were several members of the press in the room as well.

Mr. Beery opened the session by asking the audience to refrain from applauding or responding in any way to the candidates' remarks. He also said that no verbal personal attacks by the candidates would be tolerated. Then it was time for opening statements. By the toss of a coin, it had been determined that Phil Crane would go first. The representative appeared slightly nervous as he urged everyone to vote and to become politically active. "Only 29 percent of the electorate put Clinton in office," he lamented. "Remember, it was a Republican Congress that saved Social Security." Without using all of the time allotted to him for his opening statement, Crane sat down.

A Pressl supporter with a sense of humor. The "mysterious" disappearance of the "Pressl for Congress" yard signs on Lance's parents' block was reported in the Chicago Tribune, *as was this homemade replacement. Campaigns typically see these kinds of "tricks," and disappearing campaign signs is one of the oldest in the book.*

Then it was Pressl's turn. He began by thanking the AARP for providing the forum for the morning's exchange of ideas. Introducing himself as a 1975 graduate of Rolling Meadows High School, he reminded Crane of their first meeting, over twenty-five years ago. Lance then took on an urgent tone, telling the audience that there were important issues involved in this campaign, and that he and Mr. Crane differed on all of them. "This campaign is about whether we pay down the debt, which I support, or whether we give more tax breaks to the wealthy, which Mr. Crane supports. Whether we have a reliable prescription plan for seniors, which I support, or whether we continue to support special interests such as the pharmaceutical industry and the insurance companies, as Mr. Crane does. Whether funds will be available for long-term family care, which I support, or whether we worry about foreign trade, as Mr. Crane does. Whether we support funding for children at risk, which I support, or whether we oppose the Head Start Program, as Mr. Crane does. Whether we support sensible gun legislation, as I do, or whether we support the

NRA [National Rifle Association], as Mr. Crane does. Finally, whether we support meaningful campaign finance reform, as I do, or whether we collect half-million dollar contributions for our party from wealthy Silicon Valley friends in an effort to curry favor with the speaker of the House, as Mr. Crane does."

Pressl concluded his remarks by accusing Crane of having failed as a leader and having let the district down for thirty-one years. "I'm running," Lance said, "because I believe it is time for a new generation of leadership."

As Lance sat down, his supporters in the audience clapped and cheered. The Crane supporters hissed and grumbled that Lance had violated the "no personal attacks" edict. The moderator reminded Lance of the rule and, for the next hour, the candidates took turns responding to a wide range of questions.

The first question addressed government support for senior citizens. Pressl answered first, noting that the reauthorization of funds for the Older Americans Act had been languishing in Congress since 1992. "This bill contains funding for such things as nutrition for America's senior citizens. I would support that bill today," Pressl concluded.

Crane responded with an edge to his voice. "It has not been languishing since 1992. The authorization ran out and it is before the Congress now. I have supported it."

Lucia Jones, from the Agency on Aging interjected, "Yes, it has been languishing since 1992, and you have never voted for it in the past, but I'll go ahead with my next question."

The next question was put first to Crane. He was asked if he supported a ban on soft money. "Constitutionally, I believe you have a problem in banning soft money," the representative responded. "I believe in no restrictions on individual donations, but they should be reported within twenty-four hours of receipt. That would abolish soft money."

"I absolutely support a ban on soft money," Lance replied. "Mr. Crane recently collected $500,000 in soft money, and I believe he used it to buy influence with his party in the House of Representatives. I think that is deplorable. He votes against all campaign-finance reform bills."

The issues of soft money and campaign finance reform in general were hot topics in the 2000 election, as they were the centerpiece of Sen. John

The AARP sponsored a debate between Pressl and Crane (pictured here). The candidates were on opposite sides of virtually every issue. The exchange was lively and presented voters with a clear choice in the upcoming election. Crane drew chuckles from the audience near the end of the debate when, after Pressl said he would favor abolishing income tax laws that create a marriage penalty, Crane said, "we finally agree on something."

McCain's campaign against George W. Bush for the Republican presidential nomination. Amendments to the Federal Election Campaign Act of 1974, as well as various court decisions and rulings by the Federal Election Commission, created loopholes that allow campaign contributions to political parties from corporations, unions, interest groups, and wealthy individuals to be exempt from federal contribution and spending limits when that money is used for voter registration drives, efforts to increase voter turnout, and other similar activities. The funds that pass through these loopholes, commonly called "soft money" have been a target of recent campaign reform efforts.[3] The positions taken by Crane and Pressl on campaign finance reform are quite predictable, with Crane favoring a status quo approach and Pressl calling for reform.

To a question on whether Medicare benefits should extend to pre-scription drugs, Pressl said that Medicare should be extended to guar-antee money for prescriptions and that the government, including Congress, should be much more vigilant in recouping all of the money that is known to be fraudulently spent and billed under the Medicare pro-gram. Crane seemed irritated with Pressl's comment. "I believe," Crane said, "that there should be a voluntary program, in which the drug com-panies participate voluntarily, to reduce the cost of prescriptions."

And so it went. The candidates had a heated exchange about education policy and about Social Security. They disagreed about the environment and what should be done with respect to long-term care for senior citi-zens. They expressed opposing views on whether free market forces were providing adequate health care to all parts of the district and to what ex-tent material on the Internet should be filtered or censored. They differed on how to curb youth violence and on matters of foreign policy.

Finally, as the debate was drawing to a close, the candidates found some common ground. When asked about eliminating the marriage tax, Pressl said that he believed the tax should be eliminated. Crane got laughs from the audience when he said, "Lance, we are finally in agreement on something. I, too, would like to see that tax eliminated."

The Pressl team thought the debate with Crane had gone well. They were also encouraged by the remarks of Dick Kay, on-air reporter and po-litical editor at Channel 5, Chicago's NBC affiliate television station. Right after the debate, Kay was overheard commenting to a colleague that he was surprised the Eighth District race was getting so little attention. In his view, the two candidates were dramatically different, and the chal-lenger was informed and articulate. The debate received good coverage on the Channel 5 news that evening.

In general the race in the Eighth District received very little coverage on television, but in the larger scheme of congressional elections, this was not very surprising. In races where the parties are spending a lot of money, usually in a competitive race without an incumbent, television advertising can be very intense. This has the effect of making the race highly visible and can bring out the television news crews to campaign events. The Pressl campaign certainly did not have the money to do TV commercials, and help from the party for media advertising was by no means a certainty. For Crane's part, he saw no need to take his case to television, as he was already well known, and calling attention to his campaign could serve the purpose of drumming up interest in the opposition. All of these factors worked against Lance because, with the proliferation of cable stations, congressional candidates need to saturate the airwaves to be noticed. This is particularly true for the media din that characterizes a presidential election year, as was the case in 2000.

After the AARP/VOTE debate, Pressl's staff looked forward to their next chance to showcase their candidate. Later in the week Lance was scheduled to meet Crane again in an evening candidate forum that promised to draw an even larger audience.

The pace was hectic now, and there was a sense of urgency in the office about the rush to election day. Final strategies had to be developed, and more money was needed. The Pressl campaign had recently commissioned another poll of the district to get a sense of voters' reactions to the two candidates, and Lance and his team intended to base the final strategy on the poll results. The polling data gave the Pressl team hope. Voters' responses showed that positive views toward Phil Crane had declined markedly since Lance had entered the race. This provided ammunition for Lance in his effort to get financial support from the Democratic Congressional Campaign Committee (DCCC). In earlier meetings with Rep. Patrick Kennedy, the chair of the DCCC, and with Rep. Dick Gephardt, the Democratic leader in the House, Lance had been told that before party organization money would be funneled to his campaign he would need to demonstrate that he was raising a significant amount of money on his own and that there was data that substantiated his claim that he had a real chance to defeat Crane. With these latest poll results and some recent fund-raising success, the time was ripe for Lance to be in regular contact with DCCC staff in Washington, D.C., arguing that the Democratic Party pros should step up to the plate with a big infusion of money, to the tune of a few hundred thousand dollars, and the organizational expertise that would make the remaining days of the campaign as productive as possible.

Lance did call the DCCC daily and spoke to various professional staff, pleading his case and being put off to the next day or week. Claude

Walker, the more experienced of the two, doubted the party would come through. He knew that the party pros categorized elections on a three-tier model. Tier III races were those that the party saw as long shots at best and probably unwinnable. These races get little money (or none) from the party and less help in terms of personnel. Tier III races can move up to Tier II if the candidate shows that he or she is raising large amounts of money and can produce poll results indicating a decent chance of winning. If this happens, the party shows up with money and troops. Tier I races are those that the party pros believe they can win, and they literally manage the race. In Claude's view, the DCCC was likely to keep Lance at Tier III unless he brought in some big donations, and thus if they were going to win, they would have to do it without much help from the party.

While Lance worked the phones to get help from the DCCC, Claude developed an ambitious strategic plan for the last month of the race. He determined that the Pressl campaign would concentrate its efforts in the 150 precincts in which 40–50 percent of the vote had gone Democratic in the 1998 congressional election. Over two-thirds of those precincts were in Schaumburg, Palatine, and Hanover Townships; these three townships would see Pressl often in the days leading up to the election. Claude also decided that Saturday, October 14, would be Blitz Day. Volunteers were scheduled to deliver 30,000 pieces of literature to selected households, a task that would take about 600 person-hours. Volunteers would be given detailed lists of their canvassing area so that they would know which households to skip (because they had recently voted Republican) and which houses to "hit" with the brochures. One thousand yard signs touting Pressl's candidacy were also ready for volunteers to put up on Blitz Day.

The Pressl campaign also put together a printed piece entitled "Imagine." It was a three-panel brochure that featured a casual shot of Lance under block print that said, "IMAGINE, A Congressman We Can Be Proud Of For A Change." That was followed by brief biographical highlights and a list of groups endorsing his candidacy. The second panel contained six photographs, each containing a captioned message. The first three photographs were of a small boy, a young girl, and a college-age student holding textbooks. These three photographs were under

IMAGINE

A Congressman We Can Be Proud Of For A Change

Lance is a fiscal conservative and an independent Democrat. He serves as President of the Civic Federation – the nation's oldest taxpayer watchdog organization – and has dedicated himself to fighting wasteful government spending. Lance serves on the board of directors of a number of charitable groups, including Friends of Rush Children's Hospital and the Night Ministry, and served as President of the Illinois Arts Alliance.

Lance Pressl was born in Elgin, raised in Rolling Meadows and earned his Ph.D. in political science at Northwestern University. He and his wife Martha live in Rolling Meadows.

ENDORSED BY: ✔AFL-CIO ✔Illinois Federation of Teachers ✔Illinois NOW ✔American Federation of State, County & Municipal Employees (AFSCME) ✔United Auto Workers (UAW) ✔Northeast Illinois District Council of Carpenters ✔Voters for Choice ✔Sarah Brady, Handgun Control ✔UFCW ✔International Brotherhood of Electrical Workers (IBEW) ✔Sheet Metal Workers ✔Planned Parenthood ✔Citizen Action ✔and thousands of folks like you!

—— Lance Pressl for U.S. Congress ——

PAID FOR BY PRESSL FOR CONGRESS

(*Exterior*)

"IMAGINE" was one of the Pressl campaign's hard-hitting print pieces. It represents the bare-knuckled nature of the campaign in its late stages. Pressl was eager to stress issue differences that he had with Crane.

(Interior)

large block printing that said IMAGINE. The caption under the small boy read, "No Head Start Funding"; under the young girl it read, "No Department of Education"; and under the college student it read, "No College Loans." Three more photographs were side by side across the bottom of the panel. An adolescent boy, with the caption, "No Environmental Protection Laws"; a downcast thirty-something woman, with the caption, "No Ban on Assault Weapons"; and a senior citizen woman with the caption, "No Guaranteed Prescription Drug Coverage for Seniors." The two sets of pictures were separated by the following text, "Imagine if Congressman Phil Crane had gotten his way. Scary. Isn't it?" The final panel of the brochure showed a smiling Phil Crane under another bold "Imagine."

Under Crane's photo the text read, "Now imagine defeating a 31-year incumbent, anti-education, anti-gun safety, anti-environment, anti-Social Security, anti-Medicare, anti-workers' rights, the anti-choice Congressman Phil Crane. Impossible to Imagine?" The piece was hard hitting and clearly showed Lance in an aggressive campaign mode. It would be distributed in all of the door-to-door canvassing that would be done on Blitz Day and thereafter until election day.

To the extent that the candidate had time to campaign door to door, Claude determined that Lance should concentrate his effort in the twenty-five precincts with the largest percentage of Democratic voters. In addition, Pressl, as well as volunteers, would try to be available at three commuter train stations a week for each of the final four weeks of the campaign. All of the major unions represented in the Eighth District were to be contacted to find out what member-to-member communications they had undertaken or intended to do before election day. Pressl staffers would, of course, be available to help in any way they could. Lance would visit any get-out-the-vote rallies the unions wanted him to attend, and Pressl campaign volunteers would help with mailings or phone banks that the unions wanted to set up to make get-out-the-vote calls. Since the presidential race was still a toss-up, Claude was certain that the unions would be actively campaigning right up to election day, and he wanted the Pressl team to be included in any activities that the unions were engaged in.

The Pressl campaign would also set up its own six-line phone bank in Lake County and staff it with volunteers who would make calls on October 8, 9, and 10, urging people to attend a candidate forum hosted by the League of Women Voters in Arlington Heights on Friday, October 20.

Direct mailings were also part of Claude's strategy. The importance of party identification in congressional elections is considerable, often because voters possess so little information about the candidates and have only their party preferences to rely on when choosing who to vote for. Claude certainly knew how to target the mail. Every Democratic household in the district would receive a direct mail hit, as would all of the "split" households—homes in which a Democrat lived with a Republican. Households with newly registered voters or those with independent voters in precincts that were traditional Democratic strongholds were also on the direct mail list. If the campaign could afford it, targeted mailings would be sent to ethnic households, traditionally a reliable Democratic constituency. The voter file indicated that there were 8,991 households categorized as "Hispanic American" in the district, and, if the budget allowed, those households would receive a bilingual mailing featuring endorsements of Pressl's candidacy from prominent Latino leaders. Other ethnic households in the district were identified: 30,076 Irish, 9,797 Polish, 4,907 Jewish, 1,344 Asian, 1,209 Greek, and 1,196 Italian. If possible, each of these households would receive a mailing highlighting Pressl's positions on issues of concern to the targeted group.

Campaign strategy also included hiring a communications technology firm that produced and delivered "Robo-Calls." These electronically generated calls delivered a tape-recorded message from the candidate to the person answering the phone. Sunday, November 5, two days before voters went to the polls, was chosen as the day for placing 50,000 of these calls, targeted for different audiences. Democratic households in the district would get a Robo-Call message emphasizing traditional Democratic issues, such as abortion rights and gun control. A second message criticizing Phil Crane's lack of leadership and speaking of the need for change and a new vision would be directed to three additional types of households in the most heavily Democratic precincts: those with independent voters who frequently participate only in general elections, split-party households in which the residents voted in the primary election, and households with new voters. Each household scheduled for a Robo-Call was also on a list to receive a postcard no later than Friday, November 3, encouraging voters to go the polls. The card would include a photograph of Lance and a positive message.

Another part of Claude's plan for the Pressl campaign involved "human billboards." Volunteers were slated to ring bells, blow whistles, and hold large banners and homemade signs in a good-natured, attention-getting scheme near busy on-ramps and intersections in Schaumburg and Palatine townships during the morning and evening rush hours Friday, November 3, and Monday, November 6. Radio advertisements were also in the works.

As plans for the last weeks of the campaign were being finalized, the Pressl team participated in its next major public event. The League of Women Voters Forum was held at a middle school in Arlington Heights on Friday, October 20, and was also televised locally. In addition to Pressl and Crane, the two candidates for the Twenty-seventh District of the Illinois state senate participated. The forum turned into something of a free-for-all. As the *Daily Herald* reported the following day, the crowd of over one hundred "defied the moderator's entreaties not to applaud as some of the candidates mocked and berated each other." [4] The paper also reported that Pressl "called on Eighth District Rep. Philip Crane to release his income tax returns for the 31 years Crane has served in Congress, saying Crane needs to show that he has no conflicts of interest while poised to become chairman of the tax-writing House Ways and Means Committee." In addition, the story noted Lance's criticisms of Crane's actions involving campaign contributions.

One moment during the forum was especially rewarding for the Pressl camp. A member of the audience asked Representative Crane about his position on hate crimes. Crane was confused by the question, and it appeared to some members of the audience that he wasn't sure what was meant by the term *hate crimes*. When it was Lance's turn to respond, he pointed out that Crane had voted against hate crimes legislation that had been considered by the House of Representatives earlier in the fall. Pressl's reply brought cheers, hoots, and laughter from his supporters in the crowd. The Pressl team was pleased with their candidate's performance, just as they had been at the AARP debate a few days earlier.

The exchange over hate crimes was the subject of a long letter to the editor that appeared in the *Daily Herald* after the candidate forum. "Time for a change," the letter began:

I have never seen an incumbent congressman bluster through a question the way Phil Crane did at the League of Women Voters Candidates Forum in Arlington Heights on October 20.

I had asked Phil Crane and Lance Pressl a question about hate-crimes legislation. Phil Crane acted like this was the first time he had ever heard the issue.

The question was, given that hate crimes against women, including rape and domestic violence, are the most prevalent form of hate crimes in our country, what is the position of the candidates on the Hate Crimes Prevention Act, a bill that would extend existing federal hate-crimes laws to include gender among other classes. Current laws cover race, religion, and ethnicity.

Phil Crane was totally flustered by the question. He said he didn't understand the question and asked to have it repeated. He said he was not familiar with the bill. Finally, he said that, as a husband and father, he would support this bill. Lance Pressl fielded the question next. He said, "I am surprised that Congressman Crane doesn't understand the question since he voted against the bill just one month ago."

The vote on a version of that bill came up Sept. 13, and Crane did indeed vote against it. Pressl proceeded to state that he would support such a bill in a heartbeat.

Two years ago, I had asked Congressman Crane the same question at a town hall meeting in Barrington. He pleaded ignorance at that time as well. I explained to him exactly what the bill covered and how it was to be implemented. He asked his legislative assistant to make a note and to get back with me. A month later, he wrote and told me he had obtained copies of the bill in question as well as analytical material, that he had assigned it to his staff and stated, "If (the hate crimes bill) comes to the Floor of the full House of Representatives for consideration, I can cast an informed vote on (that bill) and any amendments thereto."

Crane certainly has a strange idea of "casting an informed vote" if he thinks he can vote "no" and then simply deny any knowledge of the bill. It is time to vote "yes" to Lance Pressl, a man who really does care about making informed decisions on issues that affect our lives.

M. S-M.
Arlington Heights[5]

It was flattering to have such a positive letter printed in a local newspaper. As the month of October drew to a close, however, the newspapers began printing items that were much more influential than kind words from an interested citizen. Lance and Jane and the rest of the Pressl team anxiously waited for the newspaper endorsements of candidates for various offices on the general election ballot. When the endorsements hit the newsstands, the Pressl camp found them somewhat difficult to interpret. The *Chicago Tribune,* for example, had the following to say about the Eighth Congressional District race:

> 8th District (Northwest suburbs): **Rep. Philip Crane** stunned everyone in March by admitting a problem with alcohol and taking a leave of absence for treatment. He returned invigorated and ready to battle for the chairmanship of the Ways and Means Committee. Democrat Lance Pressl is thoughtful and moderate and has a promising future.[6]

Crane's name appeared in boldface type, indicating that the *Tribune* was endorsing him. Pressl was disappointed. He had harbored some hope that one of Chicago's major dailies would endorse his candidacy. Still, there was at least a sense around the Pressl office that the paper's endorsement of Crane, a potential chairperson of a very powerful committee in the House of Representatives, was lukewarm at best.

Similarly, the *Chicago Sun-Times* offered a less-than-enthusiastic endorsement of Phil Crane while saying something positive about Lance:

> **8th:** Republican incumbent **Rep. Philip Crane** faces a credible opponent in Democrat Lance Pressl, president of the Civic Federation. But we trust that Crane's recent treatment for alcoholism will address some of his past shortcomings. He also is a contender for the powerful tax-writing chairmanship of the House Ways and Means Committee.[7]

A tepid endorsement for someone who had been in Congress over thirty years, the Pressl staff thought, but an endorsement nonetheless. Neither

Lance nor Jane could help but wonder about the nature of these two endorsements. The newspapers had both mentioned the possibility—though not the certainty—of Crane winning the chairmanship of the House Ways and Means Committee. Both papers had mentioned his recent treatment for alcoholism—typically not the sort of activity that is high on a list of reasons to recommend candidates for elective office. The Pressl team took some solace in the fact that neither paper had given a strong endorsement to Crane, nor had they mentioned a single substantive policy reason to explain their recommendations.

The Tribune and the *Sun-Times* had perhaps both witnessed enough recent history in Chicago to make courting the potential new chair of the House Ways and Means Committee just too tempting to pass up. It was less than a decade ago that Chicago representative Dan Rostenkowski had chaired the Ways and Means Committee (1984–1991) and there is no doubt that the entire Chicago area benefited from his tenure. It is a position of considerable power and the chairperson has great leverage to bargain with colleagues. The result of such bargaining, or congressional back scratching (I scratch your back, you scratch mine), can be federal grants, projects, and other pork barrel benefits that come home to the chairperson's district, and it might have been the case that the papers were viewing Crane through the same eyes that they had used to watch Rostenkowski.

The smaller, local papers brought more welcome news. *The Rolling Meadows Review* said "Send Pressl to Congress" and offered the following endorsement:

> In most situations, it would be a benefit to have your local congressman sitting in the chairman's seat of the powerful House Ways and Means Committee. But it's difficult to see how the appointment of Republican U.S. Rep. Philip Crane to this position, which could happen next year, would help the people of the 8th Congressional District.
>
> Crane is out of touch with the area's needs. He continues to repeat the same tired anti-government rhetoric he's been using for 31 years—while serving, ironically enough, in the government the entire time.
>
> How many of Crane's constituents agree with his oft-stated belief that government should be stripped down to the bare-bones functions of

defense, treasury, law-enforcement and commerce? Or with his opposition to even the most reasonable of gun-control measures?

Fortunately, voters have another choice in Tuesday's election, and they should throw their support behind Crane's Democratic opponent, **Lance Pressl.**

A fiscal and social moderate, Pressl knows the issues, thanks to his experience in state government and, more recently, as president of the Civic Federation.

Pressl wisely prefers to see the national debt paid off and Social Security and Medicare shored up before giving out the sort of reckless tax cut that Crane supports.

It's time to send someone else to Washington, and Pressl would bring a fresh perspective to the job.[8]

The *Des Plaines Journal* also offered a strong endorsement of Pressl and an equally strong repudiation of Phil Crane. The endorsement ran under the headline "Pressl Over Crane In 8th Dist." The article noted that voters in the district had a clear choice in the election: "Thirty-one year incumbent Phil Crane, a Republican who has chalked-up a record of non-accomplishment and ineffectiveness, and Lance Pressl, a savvy, articulate and knowledgeable lifelong resident of the 8th District who has solid ideas and a financially conservative outlook." The endorsement also touted Pressl's accomplishments and several of his issue stances, while referring to Phil Crane as a Washington insider who has never been known for his work ethic.[9]

The Pressl campaign could not have been more pleased with the endorsements of the two smaller papers. They knew that these small community newspapers were not without influence and that these strongly worded endorsements, coupled with the criticisms of Crane, could do nothing but help the "Pressl for Congress" effort. While there was no denying that these endorsements lacked the prestige of those given to Crane in the major dailies, the smaller local papers had loyal readerships and were widely read for the local events not covered in the big Chicago papers.

At the end of October the Pressl campaign took to the airwaves with a series of carefully placed radio advertisements. The ad spots played on two local suburban AM radio stations, as well as on WBBM, Chicago's

CBS affiliate that carried 50,000 watts of AM power with an all-news format. The ads also ran on WNUA, FM, which had a "smooth jazz" format and a large listenership among the young, upwardly mobile families that the campaign was targeting. During the final week in October and on the weekend before the election the ads aired almost constantly. They hammered hard at Crane's positions and were neither subtle nor delicate. One of them began with church bells tolling and the voices of two elderly mourners walking away from a funeral service:

FIRST VOICE: Henry was a good man.

SECOND VOICE: A real good man. A veteran too! I don't understand. How could this happen?

FIRST VOICE: He couldn't afford the medicine those doctors were prescribing. At least he had Medicare coverage and his Social Security. But he wouldn't have had those or any other benefits if Congressman Phil Crane had his way.

SECOND VOICE: How's that?

FIRST VOICE: Well, Crane wants to eliminate all kinds of federal programs. Worse yet, he thinks Medicare is a "failure" and that Social Security is a "fraudulent system."

SECOND VOICE: How can he fight for seniors when he doesn't believe in Social Security and Medicare?

FIRST VOICE: He even supports a senior prescription drug plan that's run by those big insurance companies, you know, the ones who give him campaign contributions.

SECOND VOICE: He sure isn't on our side . . . or Henry's.

FIRST VOICE: You're right . . . Henry was a good man.

SECOND VOICE: A really good man.

(musical interlude)

PRESSL'S VOICE: I'm Lance Pressl and I'm running for Congress in the Eighth District. I'll fight to save Social Security and expand Medicare to include a prescription drug program for seniors. Our seniors deserve it, and you deserve a congressman you can be proud of. I'm Lance Pressl.

MALE ANNOUNCER: Paid for by Pressl for Congress.

The second "gloves off" ad began with the sounds of birds chirping, children happily playing in a school yard and a school bell ringing in the distance. These easily recognizable sounds are abruptly interrupted by the equally recognizable sounds of automatic weapon fire, terrified screaming, and then sirens from emergency vehicles. The ad conjured up images of the April 1999 Columbine High School shootings in Colorado and asked where all the guns were coming from. It ended by noting Representative Crane's opposition to any kind of gun control legislation.

Clearly these two ads were "attack ads"—and they ran mostly through the weekend before the election. A common strategy in Chicago politics is to rough up your opponent for a couple of weeks before the election and then add your positive material to the mix just before election day.

The radio campaign concluded with a third and more positive testimonial style spot, with public figures speaking to what a fine congressman Pressl would be. One of these figures was Sarah Brady, who fought for passage of what is commonly referred to as the "Brady Handgun Control Bill" after her husband, Jim Brady, was badly wounded during the assassination attempt on President Reagan. She spoke to Lance's views on handgun control. Local environmentalists and standouts in the education community also spoke in the ad on his behalf. The spot highlighted Lance's positions and was designed to appeal to his core supporters and to any undecided moderates.

Negative campaigns have always been a part of the American political landscape, and analysis of the 2000 election demonstrates that there was certainly plenty of negativity present during that election cycle. One study showed that 91 percent of George W. Bush ads and 100 percent of Al Gore ads had a negative aspect. Another study that examined ads sponsored by interest groups found that during the last two months of the campaign, more than 80 percent of the ads sponsored by advocacy groups included something that could be considered an attack.[10] The reason for much of this negativity is no doubt linked to the theory subscribed to by most political consultants: The greater the "negatives" a candidate has the less likely he or she is to win. "Negatives" can be anything from unpopular stands on issues to poor attendance or suspect behavior on the part of office holders that can be exploited by the opposition in a campaign. There is also a belief that negative advertising, while disliked by many, is effective because it allows for dramatic commercials. Given the nature of the Eighth District race and the overall tone of the 2000 election, it is no great surprise that Pressl went negative.

The Crane campaign was also running ads, and running more of them. Rather than attack Pressl, however, Crane's ads focused on his years of congressional experience. As the incumbent with name recognition and more money than the challenger, Crane saw no reason to attack Lance. Indeed, to mention his lesser-known opponent by name would have been bad campaign strategy. Just as ads for successful commercial brand products are designed to remind buyers that the product is the one the buyers have chosen for a long time, incumbent candidates want to remind voters that the incumbent has been "tested in the market" and is the "product" voters have chosen before. Crane would gain nothing by putting Pressl's name in the minds of voters as they went to the polls on election day.

The course had been set. The race was nearly over, and Pressl was still very much the underdog. The Crane campaign did relatively little, which, depending on how you looked at it, could give Lance hope or concern. The hope could be found in thinking that perhaps he had flown below the Crane campaign's radar screen, Crane had underestimated him, and Lance would be a surprise winner on election day. The campaigning that Crane did was restricted largely to print pieces that touted his experience in Congress and all of the federal projects that he brought to the district to help improve the water and land quality. Did this mean that Crane felt vulnerable on environmental issues? Or, did so little effort by the Crane campaign indicate that Crane's years of experience had convinced him that Pressl was just another Democrat to be sacrificed? Indeed, that was cause for concern. In less than a week Lance would learn which of these possibilities, if either, was closer to reality.

The "Pressl for Congress" team continued to work hard and remained confident. They thought that their ad campaign was hard hitting and effective, and they had put together a small army of volunteers that was working tirelessly. Also, Jane's quiet confidence and steadfast belief that success is the product of hard work helped the Pressl crew press forward to election day. However, they still were concerned that they could not send as much targeted mail as they wanted, and that the DCCC had never provided support.

They would know soon how well they had done on their own.

Notes

1. Ellen Warren and Terry Armour, The INC. Column, "Parade Leaves Politician Paying Painful Price," *Chicago Tribune,* September 6, 2000.

2. Ellen Warren and Terry Armour, The INC. Column, "Political Pilferer Fails to Tear Down Sign Owner's Spirit," *Chicago Tribune,* November 7, 2000.

3. Paul S. Herrnson, *Congressional Elections: Campaigning at Home and in Washington,* 3d ed. (Washington, D.C.: CQ Press, 2000), 14–15.

4. Cass Cliatt, "Challengers Press Incumbents Crane, Jones at Voters Forum," *Daily Herald,* October 21, 2000.

5. M. S-M., "Time for a Change," Letter to the Editor, *Daily Herald,* October 29, 2000.

6. "Campaign 2000: Tribune Endorsements," Editorial, *Chicago Tribune,* October 23, 2000.

7. "Our Endorsements for the U.S. House," Editorial, *Chicago Sun-Times,* October 23, 2000.

8. "Send Pressl to Congress," *Rolling Meadows Review,* Editorial, November 2, 2000.

9. "Pressl Over Crane In 8th Dist.," Editorial, *Des Plaines Journal,* October 25, 2000.

10. Steven J. Wayne, *Is This Any Way to Run a Democratic Election?* 2d ed. (Boston: Houghton Mifflin, 2003), 187.

Election Day
The Finish Line

ELECTION DAY, NOVEMBER 7, 2000. "What a relief," Lance thought to himself as he woke up. "It's finally here." The sky was overcast, but it was not expected to rain. That was a good sign for the Pressl campaign; indeed it was good for all Democratic candidates in the region. Typically, Republicans turn out to vote at higher rates than Democrats. Turnout rates are linked to levels of education and income level, and Republicans, on the whole, tend be more highly educated and better off financially than Democrats. Because Democrats are less likely to vote, they are more apt to stay away from the polls if election day brings rain, snow, or sleet—which is not uncommon in the Northeast and Midwest. So, in addition to developing voter-registration programs, organizing get-out-the-vote efforts, and driving voters to the polls on election day, Democrats pray for dry weather. Anything that can boost turnout tends to benefit Democratic candidates.[1]

Lance and Martha drove to the polls around 9:00 a.m. On the way, Lance recounted for Martha a couple of incidents that had occurred the day before. After a typical morning of shaking hands at a commuter train station, Lance had headed over to a coffee shop in Barrington. As he sat by himself, warming up with a cup of coffee before going back to the office, Lance heard someone mention his name. He turned his head and noticed four well-dressed women sitting at a table near the window, leisurely enjoying their morning coffee and scones. They were discussing the election, and they all seemed to agree that "this young Pressl fellow" was the candidate to vote for. Lance told Martha that when he heard those women speaking so positively, he thought that there was a chance the campaign strategy had worked. As Claude had often said to Lance, "Your best bet will be to fly beneath the radar screen and sneak up on your heavily favored opponent." If these women had noticed him and planned to vote for him, Lance had thought to himself, perhaps he had done enough things right to pull off an improbable upset.

The second incident was a quick reality check. After leaving the coffee shop, Lance saw a woman and her two young children coming toward him on the sidewalk. She was just the type of voter that Lance had wanted to reach with the issues he had focused on during the long months of campaigning. He stopped and introduced himself to her, quickly pointing out the differences between his views and those of Representative Crane on education, school safety, gun violence, and the environment. The woman couldn't quite look Lance in the face. "I'm sorry," she apologized. "I've already voted absentee, and I voted Republican. I didn't know anything about you."

Lance turned to Martha. "Take your pick," he said with a grin. "Anything could happen."

Lance parked the car and they walked into his former junior high school. Today seemed different than primary election day. On that day in March, Lance had felt awkward and self-conscious about voting for himself. Today, there was no sense of uneasiness. After all he had experienced during the months of campaigning, he felt very much like a legitimate candidate whose name belonged on the ballot as the challenger to Phil Crane.

Working at the polling place was a neighbor who lived in the same condominium building as Lance and Martha. Irene was in her seventies, and she had volunteered some time to the Pressl campaign. When Irene saw Lance come into the gymnasium, she screeched, "Look, it's the cand-dee-date and Mrs. Pressl!"

Her announcement sent all of the other poll workers into a tizzy. First, the polling officials began a mad scramble to find a Mrs. Pressl in the records of registered voters, and came up empty. That's because Martha's last name is Cotton, not Pressl. That caused even more confusion with some of the older folks working at the polls, since they were not accustomed to married people having different last names. Second, when they heard that Lance was a candidate, some poll workers quickly told him that it would be unlawful for him to start campaigning there. Lance assured them that he was aware that campaigning inside a polling place was prohibited, and that he simply intended to vote and be on his way. After marking their ballots, Lance and Martha drove away from Carl Sandburg Junior High School, chuckling about the comic scene that had just been staged on this very important day.

Their next stop was the Rolling Meadows Public Library. There Lance and Martha met Lance's parents and took a couple of pictures of them as they voted for their son. They also said hello to a few of Lance's childhood friends and neighbors who, like his parents, were voting at the library. As Lance was about to leave, the father of one of Lance's fifth-grade class-mates approached him. Lance remembered the boy as someone who was always in trouble. In fact, the elementary school principal had asked Lance to walk to school with the troublemaker and keep him out of mis-chief. The father told Lance that, sadly, trouble had followed his son into adulthood. He had serious problems, including spousal abuse and drug use. Lance, while sympathizing with the father, kicked into "candidate mode" and began thinking about ways to provide people with emotional help when they need it. On a personal level, Lance felt sad for the agony that showed on the father's face. He said later, "Here's this blue collar, seventy-year-old guy, looking older than his years, devastated by what has become of his son; it certainly sounded like a plea for help. I mentioned a few social service agencies, but he had tried to contact them, and just stood there looking terribly defeated. It seemed so tragic."

The conversation resonated with Lance on a professional level as well. Early childhood intervention issues were central to his campaign, and something that he felt very passionately about. He could not help but think that any youngster who, in the fifth grade, needed to be supervised by a classmate on his walk to school should have set off bells in the mind of the elementary school principal. Could the boy have been placed in a more appropriate school or community program designed to deal with the problems that he was clearly experiencing? Lance deeply believed that such programs should be in place and should have adequate government funding.

After Lance and Martha left the library they went to "Pressl for Congress" headquarters, which was a whirlwind of activity. Volunteers were placing a final round of phone calls urging people to get out and vote. Jane was attending to some last minute arrangements for the traditional "victory" party. The Pressl team planned to gather at the Holiday Inn in Rolling Meadows, sharing a large party room with a local state Senate candidate. Jane had also booked a suite at the hotel for Lance and his family, for herself and her family, and for a few close friends. She hoped that after watching the election returns on television, they would all go down to the larger gathering and claim victory over Phil Crane.

Amid this blur of activity, Lance felt rather helpless. There really isn't much for a candidate to do as people go to the polls. The law dictates that candidates, campaign workers, and campaign materials have to remain a certain distance away from polling places. Furthermore, for every vote that might be gained by politicking on election day, another vote may be lost because the candidate looks like an undignified pest. Lance spent a short while in the office, but the staff saw his presence as a distraction. They sent him to check on turnout in a couple key precincts, and after phoning in what he learned, he went home for a few hours. There he wrote two speeches—one to be delivered if he was elected, the other to be given if the challenge failed.

Martha tried to take a nap but felt a weird anxiety. It was a bit like the butterflies she had experienced often on opening night at the theatre during her acting career, but more intense and less controllable. She wished she could do something, anything, but there really wasn't a thing she could do except wait for the election returns.

Jane's day was different than Lance's. She went straight to the office early in the morning and did not intend to go out until evening. Jane had already voted absentee so that she could be on site and available to handle anything that might arise throughout the course of election day.

There was plenty of work for Jane in the early part of the day. People who had volunteered to work election day were coming in and out, getting assignments as to which precinct they were to cover, and then heading back out to their assigned polling place. These volunteers, per Claude's plan, would introduce an old Chicago practice to the voters of the Eighth District. They would stand just outside the legal distance from the polling place and hand each voter a "palm card" as they approached. The palm card was actually a light blue slip, slightly smaller than your hand. Above a small picture of Lance it read, "A CONGRESSMAN WE CAN BE PROUD OF . . . FOR A CHANGE." Under the picture it read, "LANCE PRESSL" and below that, "Punch 24," which was Pressl's ballot position. In small print at the bottom of the palm card were Lance's endorsements and the note, "Paid for by Pressl for Congress." Frankly, Jane was a little disappointed in the number of people who showed up to work the precincts, as she expected more union people from Chicago to be out helping in the Eighth District. The scene in the office was hectic though, and the noise and the activity were somewhat therapeutic. It was also gratifying to see so much going on; Jane remembered the quiet days just after they had leased the space eleven months earlier.

Ann and Martin Ryan, the seemingly ever-present volunteers, organized a group in the office to continually make "Get out the vote" calls. These calls were carefully targeted at the most heavily Democratic precincts in the district. The field was under control, or as under control as it was going to get, and Jane had faith in Claude's plan.

Jane felt the rush of anxiety and excitement that one would expect on election day. Curiously, by late morning, Jane found herself without much to do. As she made sure everyone was on task she smiled to herself, wanting to do more, but feeling the resignation that came with knowing that she had done all she could, and now things were out of her control. After a final check with the hotel that everything was set for the victory party—the food, balloons, banners proclaiming "Pressl for Congress"— she realized that everything had been properly delegated, and now she could only wait.

As she waited, Jane was confident. She believed they were going to win. She had heard from people over and over again that Crane had been in office too long. As Jane put it, "so many people indicated that they were looking for a younger, energetic, charismatic, educated, informed, conscientious replacement. We had it all in Lance. His positions on the issues were sensitive to the needs of the people in the Eighth District. He was articulate. He listened. He cared. He was working to dedicate himself to working for the Eighth District and for the country—to make the necessary sacrifices in his personal life to represent the district in Washington."

Midday brought a couple of hopeful signs. All indications were that turnout was going to be very high. Good news for Democrats. It also appeared as though Al Gore was running very well in Lake County, which included most of the voters in the Eighth Congressional District. The Pressl team crossed their collective fingers that votes for Gore would produce a coattail effect for other Democratic candidates on the ballot. Early returns also showed that minority communities were doing a good job of getting out the vote, and if that held in the Latino areas of the Eighth District it would certainly help the "Pressl for Congress" effort. Still, there wasn't much solid information to go on, and the day seemed to drag on forever.

The earliest returns that came into the office showed Pressl leading by 2 percent. Knowing that Lance was at home and waiting, Jane called him with the news. He responded, "Well, we knew it was going to be close." The news that filtered in later was less positive. Turnout in Freemont Township, which was heavily Republican, was extraordinarily high, 70 percent, early in the day. Also, it seemed that although Lance was winning in the precincts where they expected to do well, he did not appear to be winning big, and large margins in those precincts were essential to offset the traditionally strong Republican areas if the Pressl team was going to have a chance of winning. Jane began to feel downcast as she and Claude examined the early returns. There were no further phone calls to Lance.

Mercifully, the afternoon ended, and it was time to get ready for the evening's events. As they dressed to go over to the hotel, Martha was struck at how tired and pale both she and Lance looked, how their suits seemed to hang on them. They had both lost several pounds during the campaign, and they were exhausted. But she managed to smile as they got into the car and made small talk on the way to the Holiday Inn.

Before long Lance's parents, Martha's parents, Jane and her thirty-five-year-old son, Jeff, along with his girlfriend, joined them in the living room of their suite. The room was simply furnished with chairs and a sofa covered with tired-looking fabric in somber earth tones. Lance set up his laptop on the counter that divided a kitchenette from the rest of the room.

Periodically he checked election figures provided online by the State Board of Elections. The others watched election returns on television. National media attention was focused, understandably, on the presidential race between Al Gore and George W. Bush. That contest had been too close for the political pundits to call as Americans headed to the polls that Tuesday morning, and it was still a toss-up as the polls on the East Coast began to close. In suburban Chicago, the press was most interested in the Tenth Congressional District race between Mark Kirk and Lauren Beth Gash. These two candidates were vying for an open seat that both the Democratic and Republican Parties saw as winnable; with majority control of the House of Representatives up for grabs, it was not surprising that the Democrats and Republicans had gone all out to win in the tenth.

The Kirk-Gash election was clearly a Tier I race (as discussed in Chapter 6), and it seemed to absorb all of the attention and money that was going to be heaped on House elections in suburban Chicago. Because media time, money, and party workers are all finite resources, the presence of such a hotly contested race in the neighboring district likely took away some of the attention that might have been paid to the Pressl-Crane election.

Though there was very little news about the Eighth Congressional District on television early in the evening, the Pressl team found some reason to be optimistic when, at about 7:00 p.m. central standard time (CST), the networks initially called Florida for Gore. By that time it was also clear that Hillary Rodham Clinton had won her bid to represent New York in the United States Senate, and there was talk on television of a national trend in favor of the Democrats. In fact, Lance thought he just might have done the nearly impossible. As news broke that New Jersey and Michigan, two toss-up states, had voted for Gore and television commentators began talking animatedly about a possible Democratic Party knockout, Lance found himself feeling pretty good. There was even an adrenalin-fueled smile on his face.

By 9:00 p.m., however, the mood in Lance's suite matched the somber furnishings. Some time between 8:30 and 9:00 p.m. CST Florida was taken out of the Gore column and the presidential race was deemed too close to call. Locally, news reports on television were saying nothing about the possibility of Crane not being reelected, and that would have been a stunning enough story to get mentioned on the election return coverage. Lance continued to check what returns he could find on the computer, but he was beginning to sense that the optimism of an hour ago might have been ill-founded.

Shortly after 9:00 p.m. Lance called Claude, who was holding down the fort at the "Pressl for Congress" headquarters, working the phones and computers for election returns and news. "Claude, what do you think?" he asked. Claude is a no-nonsense political pro, but he had grown genuinely fond of Lance, so there was a tinge of sympathy and some warmth in his voice, though not in the message. "It's over Lance," Claude said softly.

Lance responded, "Is there any value in holding out a while?"

"Not really," came the answer, "it's done."

The conversation was very brief. Claude would come over to the hotel shortly thereafter and join the rest of the Pressl staff for an early start on the post-mortem in the hotel bar.

As soon as Claude said there was no reason to hold out for more returns, Lance knew the race was over. He trusted Claude's instincts and experience, and Lance began thinking about moving his group out of the suite to go down to the "victory" party to thank his supporters for all their hard work and gracefully concede victory to Phil Crane.

After the conversation with Claude, Lance returned to his chair and began telling the group that it was time to think about heading downstairs to concede. The strain and disappointment showed on Lance's face as Martha stood behind his chair with her hands gently resting on his shoulders. He got up to check the latest returns on his laptop a couple more times, probably out of habit, and maybe hoping against hope that the winds would change, but the figures barely budged. It looked like Crane would garner about 60 percent of the vote to Pressl's near 40 percent. To Lance there was little consolation in the fact that Crane's 1998 opponent, Mike Rothman, managed to win only 31 percent of the vote against Crane, and Lance had bested that by nearly nine full percentage points. More clinical views of these returns would suggest that given the way things were stacked up against the Pressl team, they had actually run a surprisingly good race. But it would be some time before Lance would look at the campaign through the eyes of a political scientist. That evening he saw this particular race through the eyes of a candidate who had just been defeated.

Lance felt numb. He thought about his brother, the Labor Day parade accident, and all that he had put his family and friends through. In the background the television pundits droned on about the uncertainty of the presidential election, mirroring, in an ironic way, the uncertainty of Lance's future.

Lance's mother, Virginia, showed the same pluck that made her the aggressive signature-getter on petitions that put his name on the primary election ballot. Virginia told Lance that he had done an absolutely wonderful job and that there was no reason to rush downstairs to deliver a concession speech. Lance finally managed to quiet Virginia when he gently said, "It's over Mom. Believe me, it's over." Lance's father, Al, spoke to his son quietly, telling him how proud he was of him and how impressed he was with Lance's ability to take on such an experienced legislator.

Martha's parents, who had flown in from Boston to be with their daughter and son-in-law on election day, told Lance that he had every reason to hold his head up high. Their connections to the political world, personally and professionally, meant that they understood more than most of the guests in the room how tough a business politics is, and they knew the disappointment that Lance and Martha were feeling. Still, there was very little that they could do or say to help. They began to speak quietly of turning in soon for the night, because they had an early-morning flight back to Boston.

Shortly before 10:00 p.m. Lance picked up the phone. It was time to call Phil Crane. One of Crane's aides, Bryce Dustman, answered the call on his cell phone. Lance said hello to Bryce and asked to speak to Representative Crane. Neglecting to cover the mouthpiece of his phone, Bryce said, "Congressman, it's Lance Pressl, and he would like to speak with you."

"I'm not talking to that guy," Lance heard Crane exclaim loudly.

"Congressman, he's trying to be decent and to do the magnanimous thing and congratulate you on winning," Bryce implored. "You should speak with him."

Then Lance heard a third voice. "Just tell Pressl that Congressman Crane is busy speaking." Bryce got back on the line and repeated, "Uh, Lance, the congressman is speaking now."

Pressl sighed. "Look, Bryce, your phone has been open the entire time. I've heard everything that's been said, and learned a lot about Crane. Thank him for the education and just wish him well for me, will you?" With that, Lance hung up, shaking his head.

Jane felt hollow, empty. She will tell you without a hint of arrogance that she is simply unaccustomed to failure. She had to come to grips with the fact that they had not captured enough independent voters, nor had they caused enough defection among the Crane supporters. She was very down and would seek out her middle son, John, at the party downstairs for support. There was, she realized, some irony in the support role that her sons would play that night: All three of them, including her oldest son, Frank, worked in finance and were Republicans.

It was a quiet elevator ride down to the large room where Pressl supporters had gathered to wait for the election returns. As Lance and his family approached the room, several people stopped Lance to shake his hand or pat him on the back. Inside the party room, people were eating and drinking, watching a television in the far corner, and talking about the election. As Lance made his way to the front of the room, people began to notice him. At first they grew quiet, and then they began to clap. Lance began his short speech by telling the audience that he had just called Representative Crane to offer his congratulations. He went on to thank everyone for their hard work and support. "We almost did it," he said in a strong voice. "We managed to make a better showing than most people expected."

Lance acknowledged his family and noted how much he missed his brother Larry. Then he reminded the crowd of the important issues that had been central to his campaign and urged everyone to remain committed to the principles that had initially brought them all together. With that, the challenge to defeat Phil Crane was officially over.

As Lance started to leave the room, the crowd surged forward to shake his hand one more time, offer congratulations, and wish him well. The cheering continued until one man began chanting loudly "Pressl in '02," and others quickly joined in. Lance and Martha said a quick goodbye to their parents and left the room with the chant still ringing.

At about midnight, Jane joined Claude and the younger staff members, Mike Poleski, Jennifer Pohl, and Molly Ray, in the hotel bar. They reminisced about things that had gone on during the campaign and shared a few laughs over some of the times they had spent together. The television in the bar continued to cover the still-undecided presidential election, and while one of them would comment occasionally about how bizarre that contest appeared to be, the Bush-Gore race seemed a million miles away. They were a subdued group trying to boost each other's spirits. Jane left the bar at about 1:00 a.m. She had booked herself a room at the hotel thinking they would be up well into the morning hours celebrating and making plans to take office. Now she just wanted to go home. She was tired, knew she wouldn't sleep, but after having a couple of drinks so late, she thought better of driving home, and just went up to her room.

The next morning Lance and Martha went to Pressl headquarters. They wanted to start the process of clearing out the vestiges of the campaign. Lance was full of nervous energy as he sorted through files, deciding which ones should be kept and which ones could be thrown out. Though it seemed a bit odd to him, the phones were constantly ringing. It was almost as if the office was still open for business and yesterday's election hadn't happened. Many of the callers asked if he would be running again in two years. Lance told them he appreciated their interest, but it was much too soon to begin thinking about another campaign.

Just before lunch Lance sat down for about an hour with a few friends and a couple of key staffers to reflect on what had happened during the campaign. No longer a candidate, but rather someone with experience in running for elective office, he felt freer to talk about the ups and downs of the challenge he had undertaken. Three themes emerged in the course of the conversation: money, party support, and media.

"We never really had enough money," Lance said, "and we were always behind the eight ball when it came to funds. I do think that with more money, we could have won this race. When we went into it, I thought it would take about $600,000 to win. In the end, we had less than half of that. The professionals tell you that it takes three mass mailings for brochures and printed materials to have any real impact. We only had the money to do one. Yet after that one mailing, we had people calling the office, saying things like, 'We didn't know anything about you. What can we do to help?' That shows me that if we had had the money for more mailings, we could have made an impression on an even greater number of people who might have been convinced to vote for us."

"It also would have been nice to do some television ads," Lance continued. "I think we would have benefited from the different images that Crane and I present. And it's not just about mail and television. We certainly could have used a few more political pros, and that also takes money that we didn't have."

Lance went on to talk about the impact of party politics. "Another thing that worked against us," he stated, "was the lack of any real Democratic Party organization in this area of suburban Chicago. We had to go outside of the Eighth District and into the city of Chicago to get enough Democratic volunteers to serve as poll watchers on election day. The lack of any organized party machinery is a tremendous hindrance to anybody that is trying to defeat an entrenched incumbent. We were left to draw almost entirely on personal contacts and dedicated volunteers for help in running the campaign. A party apparatus, which has accurate voter lists and a ready-made publicity machine that can swing quickly into action, is invaluable. While Jane was pretty successful in putting together a group of Lake County Democrats who took an interest in the campaign, there just wasn't time to develop an organization that could rival that of a long-term incumbent. If the group that Jane began grows in number and level of activity between now and the 2002 election, the Democratic candidate might have some kind of a chance out here."

Finally, someone asked Lance about the press. He instinctively furrowed his brow. "There was a really bizarre disconnect between the things that reporters were saying to me and the things that were ending up in print. To my face, reporters would tell me that this is a real interesting race. With the personal problems that Crane has had, and the polar positions that he and I had on the issues, it made a great story. Moreover, they led me to believe that because of my training and background, they viewed me as a legitimate challenger to a damaged incumbent. Reporters

A large part of the Pressl team prepares for the "Unmasking Phil Crane" press conference in late October 2000. From left to right, Jane Thomas, Mike Poleski, Claude Walker (holding sign), Lance, Jennifer Pohl, and Molly Ray. The press conference was cleverly conceived, but Lance was disappointed with the coverage.

would also say to me that they were surprised at the substantive nature of various "letters to the editor" that showed this to be a race that was stirring up passion in the minds of the voters. But none of that stuff seemed to make it into print. Something weird was happening."

A puzzled look crossed Lance's face. "I remember when we did a press conference, and the title of the press conference was 'Unmasking Phil Crane.' The purpose of the press conference—held right around Halloween, and we thought that quite clever—was to expose Phil Crane's record on the issues. We produced a report card grading Phil Crane's performance in Congress."

"During that press conference," Lance reminded the group, "we also unveiled our radio ads that would be broadcast over the next several days. It seems to me that there was a substantive message about Crane's lack of attention to the district and to his responsibilities as a member of Congress being conveyed in that press conference. But the press coverage of that day focused on the theater of the event and completely failed to cover

ILLINOIS 8ᵀᴴ CONGRESSIONAL DISTRICT

REPORT CARD

Assignment: Federal Election Commission Reports (1999-00)

Name: PHIL CRANE, 8ᵗʰ District Congressman

Class Rank: 362 out of 362 (last)

Criteria:	Grade:	Comments:
Consistency	F	Phil says one thing and does just the opposite.
Thoroughness	F	Phil only completed 14% of the required work.
Accuracy	F	Phil's work shows lack of effort, 86% is missing.
Timeliness	F	Phil's report was _not_ turned in on time.
Dedication	F	Phil doesn't show any signs of motivation or concern.
Penmanship	F	Phil's reports were sloppy and handwritten.

At the "Unmasking Phil Crane" event the Pressl campaign distributed a "report card" on Crane's work, based partially on Federal Election Commission data. The message was that Crane was sloppy and that he was ignoring his responsibilities and his district.

the substance. We were providing some valuable information about Crane, corroborated by good data, and they missed the point. A couple of days later, they put us on the front page talking about how negative our radio ads were, but again, little or nothing was said about the substantive message in the ads. Now, maybe we made a mistake by doing both of those things at one press conference. In retrospect, we probably did. But we were getting so little attention from the press, we sure as heck were not about to run the risk of trying to hold two press conferences and not get any coverage at all."

In fact, Lance was probably right that there was a lack of focus to the press conference that occurred around Halloween, just before the election. The idea of "Unmasking Phil Crane" was clever, and the report card idea gave the media a single, substantive piece to consider. But by unveiling the radio ads, which would have been broadcast regardless, Lance ran the risk of losing the substantive message he hoped to send. In the end there really was nothing all that puzzling about what the press took away from the news conference; they took what they thought should be covered. Pressl gave the press a choice, they took it. By not fully controlling the message, Lance and his team allowed the press to choose what would be covered, and much to the campaign's dismay, the coverage was not at all what they wanted. Most politicians complain about press coverage, and in this instance Lance got a real lesson in why that is so often the case.

Lance was quiet for a moment. "Yes, I'm disappointed in the press, but I can't make the press the scapegoat and blame them for our defeat. But I'll always be puzzled by the way the press treated our campaign."

There would be more time for reflection, and time to figure out what to do next. But now it was time to go home and pack for a few days away from Chicago's November cold. Lance and Martha were ready for an agenda that included nothing more than relaxing on a warm beach. Lance looked tired, but not particularly downcast. The events leading up to election day had probably prepared him better for disappointment than he possibly could have imagined.

The "Pressl for Congress" campaign fits the pattern of congressional elections very well. Feisty challengers, no matter how well qualified, well intentioned, or attractive, cannot reasonably expect to have much success against a long-term incumbent. The problems that plagued the Pressl campaign—low visibility, lack of party support, funding shortages, and difficulty getting public exposure—are common to the vast majority of campaigns waged by challengers against incumbents for seats in the House of Representatives. The same patterns hold in most elections for state and local offices as well. However, the political pros and the politicians themselves will tell you that there's always the possibility, no matter how minuscule, that a savvy challenger could sneak up on an incumbent, the media, and anyone else who might not be watching very carefully, and put an underdog in office.

Note

1. For a discussion of voter turnout, see John F. Bibby, *Politics, Parties, and Elections in America*, 4th ed. (Belmont, Calif.: Wadsworth, 2000), 312–323.

Epilogue
New Challenges

THE ELECTION OF 2000 was one of the most interesting elections in decades. The television networks projected presidential winners only to retract those projections throughout election night. Disputed votes in Florida gave rise to numerous proceedings in the state and federal courts. It took a decision by the United States Supreme Court in December 2000 to end the uncertainty about who the next president would be, though the Court's ruling by no means ended the controversy. In the end George W. Bush's 271 electoral votes bested Al Gore's 266, though Gore had won more popular votes than Bush. In Congress the Republicans retained control of the House by a slim margin, whereas the Senate was evenly divided—fifty Republicans, fifty Democrats. This unusual split ended in May 2001 when Sen. James Jeffords of Vermont, in an equally unusual move, announced that he was leaving the Republican Party. Though Jeffords became an independent, he declared that he would sit with the Democratic Caucus, giving Democrats control of the Senate by one vote. From these events we can see that much of what happened on the national political scene in the days and months following November 7, when voters went to the polls to cast their votes, was simply unpredictable.

The outcome of the race in the Eighth Congressional District of Illinois, on the other hand, was entirely predictable, and it was an outcome that was replayed in most of the congressional districts across the country. Of the 403 incumbents who ran for reelection to the House of Representatives in 2000, 394 (98 percent) won. Only six incumbents seeking reelection were defeated in the general election; three others lost in primary elections to challengers from their own parties.[1]

As the country moved into a new millennium, the lessons of the House races during the 2000 election cycle remained rooted in the past. Challengers, who for months had been active, visible candidates on the campaign trail, were, in the span of a few hours on election night relegated to the category of "also ran." Simply put, incumbents usually win—and win big. The final numbers in the Eighth District showed Crane winning with 61 percent of the vote to Pressl's 39 percent.[2] Nationwide, 77 percent of the incumbents won reelection with 60 percent or more of the vote.[3]

As Lance's campaign makes all too clear, one of the reasons incumbents are difficult to beat is their ability to raise money. Typically, they outspend their opponents by a margin of more than two to one. Election year 2000 was no different. In that year the average incumbent spent $814,507; the average challenger spent $369,823.[4] Phil Crane raised $1,059,548 and spent $932,174 on the campaign. PACs contributed 64 percent of the money that went into Crane's campaign war chest. None of the money that Crane raised came from his personal accounts. Pressl, on the other hand, spent $242,501. PAC contributions accounted for a mere 16 percent of the total $280,017 that the Pressl campaign was able to raise, while 33 percent ($92,431) came from the candidate himself.[5] Although the Crane campaign was invisible throughout most of our story, Crane still managed to raise and spend more money than Pressl did, and in a shorter time. Targeted mailings are expensive, as are radio time and production. Crane's campaign finances illustrate that not only are incumbents successful fundraisers, but they know how to effectively spend what they raise.

In Pressl's case there was a brief glimmer of hope with respect to a large PAC cash infusion slightly less than two weeks before election day. As Lance was driving to an evening event he got a call on his cell phone from the head of the local carpenters' union. The union official sounded very excited and told Lance that he had finally convinced the Democratic Congressional Campaign Committee to put some money into the Illinois Eighth District race. Lance was told to expect a call early the next day. He thanked the local union official profusely and began thinking about where to spend the money. More radio? TV? Was it too late to do another mail piece? He would talk to Claude as soon as he could. However, the call from the "D Triple C" never came and any thoughts Lance had about how to spend the money were moot. It is probably not uncommon for long-shot challengers to experience this kind of disappointment. This example also illustrates how difficult it is for challengers to raise money.

There is no question that some of the Pressl campaign's chronic underfunding was a result of never receiving help from the Democratic Party organization or many prominent Democrats. During the summer, Rep. Barney Frank, D-Mass., spoke at a fund-raiser for Lance, and with about ten days to go in the campaign Rep. Jesse Jackson Jr., D-Ill., and Rep. Rod Blagojevich, D.-Ill., who would be elected governor of Illinois in 2002, spoke at a fund-raiser and rally in support of Lance. Despite these high-profile supporters, the Pressl campaign never got beyond the Tier III classification of the party and thus labored in relative obscurity. Moreover, a candidate can have all of the high-profile support in the world, but if that support is not covered heavily in the local media, it is not likely to make that much difference, particularly if the support is lent to somebody running against a longtime House incumbent.

Another advantage incumbents have, of course, is name recognition. Lance became painfully aware of that throughout the campaign—and even on the day before the election, when that young woman he met on the street in Barrington confessed, "I've already voted absentee . . . I didn't know anything about you." Because the press does not cover challengers very much, lack of name recognition is likely to be enough to doom a challenger's campaign. As Paul Herrnson writes, "Press coverage in House contests between an incumbent and challenger is so unequal that veteran Democratic political adviser Anita Dunn believes 'the local press is the unindicted co-conspirator in the alleged "permanent incumbency." ' As Dunn explains, 'A vicious circle develops for challengers—if early on, they don't have money, standing in the polls, endorsements, and the backing of political insiders, they—and the race—are written off, not covered, which means the likelihood of a competitive race developing is almost nonexistent.' " [6]

That's not to say that press coverage of Phil Crane was very positive. Much of it was anything but. The *Chicago Tribune* ran a story less than two weeks before the election that most would consider devastating to someone who was in the midst of a campaign for high elective office. It began,

> ... one day in March, at about 3 p.m., eight confidants gathered in Rep. Phil Crane's office to make the Illinois Republican see himself like many on Capitol Hill did, as a conservative stalwart whose personality, political energy and brilliant grasp on tax issues had been clouded by years of drinking. . . . Crane, the most senior Republican in the House, had been on a political road to nowhere for much of the last decade. His northwest suburban district is faithfully Republican, so he had little trouble winning re-election over and over despite his inattentiveness on the job. . . . Now, as the election approaches, Crane's friends acknowledge that his willingness to accept their intervention was as much pragmatic as personal: A powerful House leadership position was finally within reach after 31 years in Washington. Those friends convinced Crane on that March afternoon that the biggest obstacle to achieving that goal was his penchant for drinking up to 10 Heinekens a night. Crane would often tote his own beer to events, just in case his favorite brand wasn't served. He would stand in the corner at social functions . . . and become more withdrawn with every fresh green bottle he cracked open. . . . So during that 90-minute meeting March 21 . . . Crane pored over his schedule and insisted he was too busy to spend a month in a secluded rehabilitation center. But his daughter, former staff members and friends wouldn't relent. They told Crane if the alcohol didn't kill him, it would end his chances of becoming chairman of the House Ways and Means Committee, one of the most powerful positions on Capitol Hill. If he wanted to salvage his health and renew his political life, his friends said, he must seek treatment and publicly admit what everyone already knew.[7]

Indeed, Crane broke the news to his colleagues in a letter, saying, "Over a period of time, I have sensed an increased dependence on alcohol. This dependence has taken a toll on my health and other aspects of my life."[8]

We noted earlier that the playing field is not level when it comes to press coverage of incumbents and challengers, but in view of the treatment of Representative Crane illustrated above, we might question just how relevant the press is at all in congressional elections. Because so many people cannot name their own House member, and so few have any idea what is going on in Congress, the press has a small audience for an article like this. Moreover, since trust in the media is low, we can wonder whether a piece like this has any impact at all. It is likely that the article could have led Crane supporters to disregard the story as hyperbole and allowed Crane detractors to continue to hold negative views of him. A highly negative article like this brings to mind the view that the Reagan White House took of the press: Coverage of any sort is good coverage. The fact that Crane's name was in the press at all probably reinforced his position as a newsmaker. Lance, though he did not receive bad press, was at a more serious disadvantage: he was apparently *not* a newsmaker. If there's no such thing as bad press, negative pieces about the incumbent are unlikely to have much impact, particularly in the absence of highly positive pieces about a little-known challenger. In the final analysis though, name recognition probably trumps the media as a cue to which voters respond, which, as we have noted, is almost always going to favor the incumbent.

Constituents also are often reluctant to gamble on a challenger, because to do so is to relinquish any power or influence that may come to an incumbent through seniority or experience. Thus it is no small irony that the power and influence that Crane's position promised on the eve of the election never actually came to be. When the 107th Congress convened in January 2001, Rep. Bill Thomas of California was named the new chair of the Ways and Means Committee, not Phil Crane. "Crane Fails to Win Key House Post" headlined a page-one story in the *Daily Herald* after the Republicans reconvened as the majority party in the House of Representatives.

> Congressman Philip M. Crane's 30-year road to the House Ways and Means chairmanship came to an abrupt dead end Thursday when Republican colleagues—including Speaker Dennis Hastert—failed to back him for the post he coveted.
>
> Hastert, like Crane a suburban [Illinois] Republican, said he chose to support Crane's main opponent, Rep. Bill Thomas of California, because Thomas had the "expertise and ability" for the job.[9]

The story also noted that a Republican insider had suggested that Republican colleagues may have felt that Crane, who had gone through a month-long alcohol rehabilitation program in 2000, was not up to the daunting tasks facing the Ways and Means Committee chair.

The *Daily Herald* story was followed by a piece in the Commentary section of the Sunday edition of the *Chicago Sun-Times*. In "Sloth, Thy Name Is Phil Crane: The Ways and Means Post Is Out of Reach after Many Ineffective Years in Congress," *Sun-Times* columnist Steve Neal wrote that Crane was passed over for the chairmanship "for the simplest of reasons. He is a legislative lightweight who lacks the stature for the job." Neal went on to state, "Crane has an aversion to hard work." After Crane's poor showing in his bid to win the GOP presidential nomination in 1980, he "virtually retired from his congressional seat," though "he didn't bother to inform his constituents, and has retained the title." [10] The following Tuesday, January 9, the *Chicago Tribune* also weighed in with an editorial suggesting that while it would have been good for Illinois to have one of its own chair the Ways and Means Committee, "it's hard to shed a tear over what happened. Crane didn't earn the job. He has few legislative accomplishments and for years all but ignored his suburban district." [11]

Lance Pressl reacted to the news of Crane's failure with a combination of vindication and anger. "I wasn't surprised that he was passed over for the chairmanship of Ways and Means," Pressl later said. "He didn't get the post because he has not been a good legislator. I said that during the campaign and I still think that it is the case. The fact that Crane did not get a single vote from his party, and his colleague from Illinois, Speaker of the House Dennis Hastert, turned his back on him kind of put an exclamation point on everything I had ever said about Crane."

At the same time, Pressl's anger was also directed at the editorial boards of the *Tribune* and *Sun-Times*. He was bothered that each had held out the possibility that Crane might get the coveted chairmanship in their endorsements, because many insiders were very doubtful that it would happen. Pressl wondered if the major dailies were actually that far out of the loop (which, frankly, he doubted), or just not willing to risk their endorsements and alienate Crane. He also thought the papers' repudiation of Crane after he failed to get the chairmanship was late and little more than the papers "covering their own backsides." However, Pressl realized that he probably still would not have won had he gotten the papers' endorsements.

Throughout the winter of 2001 there was speculation that Crane would choose to end his congressional career by not seeking reelection the following year. Others suggested that if he decided to run, he might get beaten. Political observers were interested in how Crane's district was going to be reconfigured, since Illinois had lost one House seat following the decennial census. Redistricting could be an important factor in determining Crane's political future. But when the Illinois congressional districts were redrawn in the spring of 2001, the representative could not have been put in a better position. In fact, the Eighth District had been newly drawn in a way so favorable to Phil Crane that it was covered on the front page of the *Chicago Tribune.*

> Lance Pressl campaigned hard against U.S. Rep. Phil Crane, R-Ill. last year and hoped to run against the incumbent again in 2002. But when the new congressional districts were approved last month, Pressl found that he had been drawn out of Crane's 8th Congressional District, which now ends about 50 feet from Pressl's Rolling Meadows condominium.[12]

Indeed, as both the *Tribune* and the *Daily Herald* noted, the residences of two other former challengers to Crane were also "mapped out" of the district. David McSweeney, who faced Crane in the Republican primary in 1998, and Gary Skoien, Crane's opponent in the GOP primary in 1992 and 1994, found themselves, along with Pressl, in the new Tenth District.[13]

In 2002 Crane, now in his early seventies, ran for reelection to Congress. He faced another Democratic newcomer, businesswoman and high-tech company consultant Melissa Bean. Crane outspent Bean by a margin of more than two to one and won handily—57 percent to 43 percent. Phil Crane returned to Washington, D.C., to the job he has held for nearly thirty-five years.

Washington, D.C., is also home now to Lance Pressl and Martha Cotton. After losing the challenge to Crane in the Eighth District, Lance took a position in government relations with an organization representing the interests of institutions of higher education across the country. Martha's design research firm easily accommodated her transfer from Chicago to their Washington office. New and exciting challenges came their way with the birth of a son in December 2001.

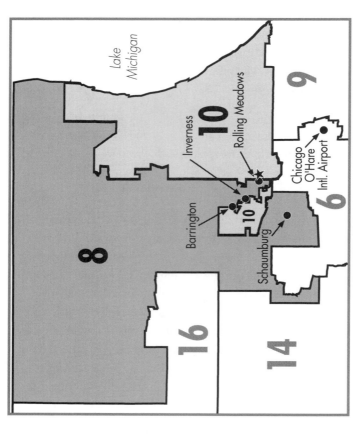

The Eighth Congressional District in Illinois, 2002. Note that Lance has been mapped out of the district by a matter of feet (his condominium is indicated by the star in the map). He was not alone in being treated to the time-tested practice of gerrymandering, or drawing political boundaries for the benefit of a party or candidate. Two of Representative Crane's other recent opponents also were drawn out of the district. All three past candidates found themselves in the newly configured Tenth District.

Every day as Lance drives to work he glances up at the Capitol dome. Does he regret running for the House of Representatives? "Not at all," he responded when I asked.

"Do you still harbor a desire to serve in Congress?" I pressed. Lance's reply came without a moment's hesitation. "Absolutely."

Pressl's reaction is interesting, and while he is currently living in Washington, D.C., and therefore cannot run for Congress as a voting member, it is testimony to the strength of the congressional tradition that he would still like to serve. There are certainly imperfections in the system, but its ability to generate challengers speaks volumes to the fact that there is always the possibility for a challenge like Pressl's to be successful.

Finnegan Pressl, at age one and a half years, is pictured here on the steps of the Cannon Office Building on Capitol Hill. One could imagine this sort of photograph sitting on the desk of a representative in office. What will Finnegan eventually take away from his father's experience on the campaign trail? Will he want to pursue a career of public service? Much could depend on the course of campaign and congressional politics in the years to come.

Notes

1. Norman J. Ornstein, Thomas E. Mann, and Michael J. Malbin, *Vital Statistics on Congress: 2001–2002* (Washington, D.C.: AEI Press, 2002), 69.

2. Center for Responsive Politics, www.opensecrets.org/2000elect/disttotal/IL08htm.

3. Ornstein, Mann, and Malbin, *Vital Statistics,* 75.

4. Ibid., 87.

5. Center for Responsive Politics, www.opensecrets.org/2000elect/disttotal/IL08htm.

6. Paul S. Herrnson, *Congressional Elections: Campaigning at Home and in Washington,* 3d ed. (Washington, D.C.: CQ Press, 2000), 216.

7. Jeff Zeleny, "Sober Crane Has Life, Clout Back, Friends Say," *Chicago Tribune,* October 27, 2000.

8. Ibid.

9. Eric Krol, "Crane Fails to Win Key House Post: Hastert Passes on Veteran to Lead Ways and Means," *Daily Herald,* January 5, 2001.

10. Steve Neal, "Sloth, Thy Name Is Phil Crane: The Ways and Means Post Is Out of Reach after Many Ineffective Years in Congress," *Chicago Sun-Times,* January 7, 2001.

11. "The Repudiation of Phil Crane," Editorial, *Chicago Tribune,* January 9, 2001.

12. Dan Mihalopoulos, "Political Opponents Cast Out by Remap," *Chicago Tribune,* June 27, 2001.

13. Ibid.; and Eric Krol, "New Map a Gift for Crane," *Daily Herald,* June 27, 2001.

Index

Page numbers in **bold** indicate photographs. Note references include "n" after page numbers.

Campaigning *(continued)*
  staff, 21
  summer campaign trail, 67–72, 77–95
  volunteers. *See* Volunteers
Candidate-centered campaign, 36
Candidates. *See also* Crane, Phil; Pressl,
  Lance
  amateurs, 14
  announcement of candidacy, **11,**
    41–45, **42**
  appeal of, 65
  campaign professionals, relation-
    ship with, 65
  fund raising by. *See* Fund raising
  personal and strategic qualities of,
    14, 74–75
  "pros," 14
  psychological characteristics com-
    mon to, 73–74
Celebrities as members of Congress, 75
Center for Responsive Politics, 148*n*
Challenger's decision to run, 7–22
Cheney, Dick, 91
Chicago Civic Federation, 9, 17, 35,
  36, 46
China-U.S. trade relations, 43–44
Cliatt, Cass, 122*n*
Clinton, Bill, 13, 25, 52
Clinton, Hillary Rodham, 129
Coffees, 101, **102**
Committee chair system, 46–47. *See
  also* Ways and Means Committee
  chairmanship
Committees. *See* Democratic Congres-
  sional Campaign Committee
  (DCCC); Political action commit-
  tees (PACs)
  House Committee. *See* Ways
    and Means Committee
    chairmanship
Communications technology firm,
  hiring of, 113
Community groups, speaking engage-
  ments at, 41, 100–101
Community technology firm, 113
Concession by candidate, 131–132

Congratulation-rationalization effect,
  73–74
Congress
  circle of support for members, 18–19
  committee chair system, 46–47
  Ways and Means Committee. *See*
    Ways and Means Committee
    chairmanship
  well-known public figures as
    members, 75
Consultants, 65. *See also specific consultant by name*
  campaign professionals, 52–53
  clashes with, 65
  communications technology firm,
    113
  field director, 77, 99–100
  fund raising, 61
Cotton, Clare, 51
Cotton, Martha (wife of Lance Pressl),
  7, **11, 19,** 79
  announcement of candidacy and,
    41–42
  decision to run and, 17–18
  education and career of, 18, 145
  gathering signatures by, 37
  support of candidacy by, 17–18, **19,**
    73
  voting on election day, 123–125
Crane, Arlene, 29
Crane, Dan, 13, 28
Crane, George, 28
Crane, Phil (incumbent opponent), **16,
  21,** 34*n*
  advertising by, 121
  at parade, **69**
  campaigning by, **32,** 91, 121
  China insult, 43–44, **44**
  debate, 71, 103–107, **106**
  differences from Pressl, 27–28,
    31–34, 50, 81–82
  drinking problem of, 12, 14, 55–56,
    142
  education and career of, 28–30
  high school meeting with Pressl,
    15–16, **16,** 46